The Facts and Fictions of Minna Pratt

§§

PATRICIA MacLACHLAN

A Charlotte Zolotow Book

HARPERTROPHY®
AN IMPRINT OF HARPERCOLLINS *PUBLISHERS*

Special thanks to three people—
To Sally Bagg for years of earnest and enthusiastic talk
of music and its drama;
To Jane Carnes for a quiet place to write
and the nurturing that came with it;
To Jason Melanson for the young unfettered wisdom
that many of us have forgotten.

Harper Trophy® is a registered trademark of
HarperCollins Publishers Inc.

The Facts and Fictions of Minna Pratt

For information address HarperCollins Children's Books,
a division of HarperCollins Publishers,
1350 Avenue of the Americas, New York, NY 10019.

Library of Congress Cataloging-in-Publication Data
MacLachlan, Patricia.
    The facts and fictions of Minna Pratt.
        p.   cm.
    "A Charlotte Zolotow book."
    Summary: An eleven-year-old cellist learns about life from her
eccentric family, her first boyfriend, and Mozart.
    ISBN 0-06-024117-9 (lib. bdg.) — ISBN 0-06-440265-7 (pbk.)
    [1. Musicians—Fiction.]   I. Title.
PZ7.M2225Fac   1988   85-45388
[Fic]   CIP
                                                     AC

Typography by Bettina Rossner
First Harper Trophy edition, 1990
Visit us on the World Wide Web!
www.harperchildrens.com

Once I told a class of Natalie Babbitt's that she had inspired and encouraged me as a writer, as a friend. "Why, then," said Natalie crisply (joking, of course), "haven't you ever dedicated a book to me?" Well, this is it, with deep affection.

To Nat from Pat

We all know that art is not truth.
Art is a lie that makes us realize the truth.
—Pablo Picasso

ONE

Melinda Pratt rides city bus number twelve to her cello lesson, wearing her mother's jean jacket and only one sock. Hallo, world, says Minna. Minna often addresses the world, sometimes silently, sometimes out loud. Bus number twelve is her favorite place for watching, inside and out. The bus passes cars and bicycles and people walking dogs. It passes store windows, and every so often Minna sees her face reflection, two dark eyes in a face as pale as a winter dawn. There are fourteen people on the bus today. Minna stands up to count them. She likes to count people, telephone poles, hats, umbrellas, and, lately, earrings. One girl, sitting directly in front of Minna, has seven earrings, five in one ear. She has wisps of dyed green hair that lie like forsythia buds against her neck.

There are, Minna knows, a king, a past president

of the United States, and a beauty queen on the bus. Minna can tell by looking. The king yawns and scratches his ear with his little finger. Scratches, not picks. The beauty queen sleeps, her mouth open, her hair the color of tomatoes not yet ripe. The past president of the United States reads *Teen Love* and *Body Builder's Annual*.

Next to Minna, leaning against the seat, is her cello in its zippered canvas case. Next to her cello is her younger brother, McGrew, who is humming. McGrew always hums. Sometimes he hums sentences, though most often it comes out like singing. McGrew's teachers do not enjoy McGrew answering questions in hums or song. Neither does the school principal, Mr. Ripley. McGrew spends lots of time sitting on the bench outside Mr. Ripley's office, humming.

Today McGrew is humming the newspaper. First the headlines, then the sports section, then the comics. McGrew only laughs at the headlines.

Minna smiles at her brother. He is small and stocky and compact like a suitcase. Minna loves him. McGrew always tells the truth, even when he shouldn't. He is kind. And he lends Minna money from the coffee jar he keeps beneath his mattress.

Minna looks out the bus window and thinks about her life. Her one life. She likes artichokes and blue fingernail polish and Mozart played too fast. She loves baseball, and the month of March because no one else much likes March, and every shade of brown she has ever seen. But this is only one life. Someday, she knows, she will have another life. A different one. A better one. McGrew knows this, too. McGrew is ten years old. He knows nearly everything. He knows, for instance, that his older sister, Minna Pratt, age eleven, is sitting patiently next to her cello waiting to be a woman.

"Unclothed Woman Flees from Standard Poodle," sang McGrew, reading the headlines. "Boa Constrictor Lives in Nun's Sewing Basket. Sit down, Minna Pratt," he sang on.

"Hush up, McGrew," said Minna. "A mysterious woman just got on the bus. Number fifteen."

"Mysterious how?" sang McGrew, ending on a high note just above his range.

"A fur cape, gray braids, one earring," said Minna. "That makes seventeen earrings total on this bus."

"Emily Parmalee just got her ears pierced," said McGrew in his speaking voice. "She's meeting us at the bus stop."

Minna snorted, but not unkindly. Emily Parmalee was the catcher on McGrew's baseball team. She was, like McGrew, small and squat, with an odd sense of humor. Often she caused Minna to laugh so hard that she had to lie down on sidewalks or crouch in soda shops. Minna smiled, thinking enviously of Emily Parmalee, rushing toward womanhood faster than Minna, her ears already past puberty.

The bus jolted to a stop and Minna leaned her head against the window and thought about her lesson. Minna never practiced, except for the short times when everyone was out of the house. When no one was there, she could play bad notes without anyone calling out or McGrew humming them in tune as a guide. Minna never needed to practice, really. She could, in the presence of her cello teacher, Mr. Porch, summon up the most glorious notes; pure, in fact, surprising even Minna. She played beautifully for Mr. Porch, mostly because she wanted to make him smile, as somber as he sometimes was. Also, she felt sorry about his name. Porch. Verandah might have been better. Or even Stoop. Porch was a dismal name. For a sometimes dismal man. McGrew called him Old Back.

Someone pulled the bell cord and it was their stop. McGrew folded his newspaper under his arm, reaching over to the seat across the aisle to snatch *The Inquirer,* forbidden at home even though it had the best headlines. Minna propped her cello on her hip and pushed through the crowd.

"Pardon. I'm sorry. Excuse."

The beauty queen woke up, closing her mouth and gathering packages. The past president of the United States put *Teen Love* and *Body Builder's An-*

nual carefully between the pages of his *Atlantic Monthly*. The king scratched on.

Emily Parmalee was at the bus stop with the shirt of her long underwear worn on the outside and brand-new holes in her ears.

"McGrew!"

"Emmy!"

They always greeted each other as if they had been lost on the prairie, smiles and exclamation points. A matched pair of luggage, thought Minna.

"Hallo, Emily," said Minna. "I like your ears."

Emily Parmalee grinned.

"I'll have feathers within the month," she said matter-of-factly.

Minna pulled her cello up the steps to the conservatory. The sky was gray, with low clouds, like in an old painting.

"I'll be forty-five minutes today, an hour at the most," Minna called.

"That's all Old Back can take," said McGrew, sitting down and taking a very black banana out of his jacket pocket.

On this dismal day Minna Pratt, cellist, climbs the steps to her dismal lesson with her sometimes dismal teacher, Porch. Outside sits McGrew with a dismal banana. And Emily Parmalee, who does not yet have feathers. Dismal is all Minna can think of. A dismal life. But she is wrong. Old Back Porch has a surprise for her. The surprise is not Mozart. The surprise is not dismal. It is Lucas, tall and homely and slim with corn-colored hair. With blue eyes, one that looks off a bit to the side. And with a wonderful vibrato.

TWO

Minna paused before the great wooden door of the conservatory and looked up for good luck to where the gargoyles rested, gray and ominous and familiar. Then she pushed open the door and began the walk up the three flights of stairs. There was an elevator, but it was self-service, and Minna had nightmares of being stuck there between floors with no one to talk with, nothing to count. Alone with her cello. Minna, of course, would not practice.

> TV ANNOUNCER: *"After three days and two nights of being stranded in an elevator, Minna Booth Pratt has emerged, blinking and looking rested."*
> MINNA: [*Blinking and looking rested.*]
> TV ANNOUNCER: *"A record, ladies and*

*gentlemen! Seventy-two hours in an elevator
without practicing!"*
[*Applause, applause, cheering.*]

Sighing, Minna paused at the first-floor landing
to look out the window. Below were McGrew and
Emily Parmalee, slumped over like half-filled travel
bags, singing. Minna pulled her jacket around her,
the chill of the old building numbing her fingers.
Far off she heard an oboe playing Ravel, a sound
as sad and gray as the building. She walked up the
last flight of stairs, slowly, slowly, thinking of yesterday's lesson. It was Bartók, bowing hand for
Bartók staccato; swift, short bows, Porch's hand
on her elbow, forcing her wrist to do the work.
When she got it right, he would smile his Bartók
smile: there quickly, then gone. It would be early
Haydn today. High third finger, she reminded herself, digging her thumbnail into the finger, forcing
it to remember. After Haydn it would be the Mozart. *The Mozart. K. 157.* The number was etched
on her mind, and Minna stopped suddenly, her
breath caught in her throat. The Mozart with the
terrible andante she couldn't play. The andante her
fingers didn't know, *wouldn't* know. And then the
wild presto that left her trembling.

Minna shook her head and walked on. Today
was chamber group, three of them, with Porch, the
fourth, playing the viola part. Called chamber group

by all but Porch, who referred to it as "mass assembled sound."

Minna would be late. She was always the last one to arrive, no matter what early bus she took. Everyone would be there, Imelda and Porch; Orson Babbitt with his tight black curls and sly smile. Minna pushed the door open with one finger and they were tuning, Porch scuttling sideways like a crab between music stands with an armful of music. Imelda stopped playing and laid her violin on her lap, one foot crossed primly over the other, her black braids slick as snakes.

"It's three thirty-five," she announced, glancing at the clock. "And you've got only one sock."

"That's in case you care," said Orson, making Minna grin.

Imelda was touched with perfect pitch as well as other annoyances. She pronounced varied facts even when not asked. She could recite the kings of England in order, backward and forward, the dates of major gang wars, important comets, what mixtures produced the color mauve. Imelda: fact gatherer, data harvester, bundler of useless news.

"It's WA today, Minna," called Orson from across the room, Orson's name for Wolfgang Amadeus Mozart. Orson played second violin with a sloppy serenity, rolling his eyes and sticking out his tongue, his bowing long and sweeping and beautiful even when out of tune. "If you must make a mistake," he had quoted, "make it a big one." Was it Heifetz who had said it? Perlman? Zukerman maybe?

"Tune, tune," said Porch briskly. He turned to Orson. "And is there a word for today?" Orson was the word person, spilling words out as if they were notes on a staff.

"Rebarbative," said Orson promptly. "Causing annoyance or irritation. Mozart's rebarbative music causes me to want to throw up."

Porch sighed. Orson preferred Schubert.

Suddenly Porch brightened, looking over Minna's head.

"Ah, good. I'd nearly forgotten. There is an addition to our group. A newcomer."

Everyone looked up. Minna turned.

"This is Lucas Ellerby," announced Porch, beckoning him in. "Lucas will play viola with us from now on."

The boy paused at the doorway. His hair fell over his forehead.

"Imelda and Orson," introduced Porch. "Minna Pratt, too."

Minna smiled. It sounded like the beginning of a nursery rhyme she half remembered:

Imelda and Orson and Minna Pratt, too,
Set out in a gleaming bright boat of blue. . . .

"Lucas will play viola next to Minna," Porch went on. "I'll play first with Imelda. Trying hard not to be rebarbative."

Lucas smiled for the first time.

"That bad?" he asked.

Orson looked up quickly. There was a silence while Lucas unlocked his case and took out his viola and bow. Finally Imelda spoke.

"Have you heard the fact," she asked, her eyes bright, "that the great wall of China is actually visible from the moon?"

A fact, thought Minna. A mauve fact might follow.

Lucas sat down next to Minna.

"Yes," he said simply. He smiled a radiant sudden smile at Imelda as he tightened his bow. "Wonderful, yes? A fine fact."

Minna watches Lucas's long fingers curl around his viola, one leg stretch out, one slide back to hook over a chair rung. There is a grand silence as they all stare at Lucas. Minna does not fall in love quickly. Most often she eases into love as she eases into a Bach cello suite, slowly and carefully, frowning all the while. She has been in love only once and a half. Once with Norbert with the violent smile who sells eggs from his truck. The half with one of her father's patients, a young man who made her breathless with his winks. When she discovered he also winked at her mother, father, McGrew, and the car, she slipped backward out of love again.

"Scales first," said Porch. "Old, familiar friends, scales. G to start."

They played scales, staring at nothing, no music needed because Porch was right . . . the scales were old friends.

"Now," said Porch, "let's begin with something we know. Mozart, K. 156. Presto, but not too presto." He raised his violin. "An A, everyone." They played an A, Orson making gagging noises.

Old Back lifted his bow.

The great wall of China, thought Minna. A fine fact.

"Ready," said Porch.

I wish I'd thought of that fine fact. Then Lucas would have smiled at me.

"Here we come, WA," said Orson softly.

"High third finger, Minna," whispered Porch.

And they play. They begin together and Minna holds her breath. Often they stumble into the music, Porch louder, counting; Imelda scowling and playing too fast; Orson snorting in rhythm. But today is different. They begin on the same note and play together. In tune. Minna looks at Porch and sees that he has noticed the difference, too. Lucas's hand vibrates on the strings. They all hear the strong, rich sound of his vibrato. Lucas peers at Minna and grins. And suddenly Minna realizes that she is smiling. She has never smiled through an entire movement of WA Mozart. Ever.

"Splendid, splendid," said Porch, gathering up the music. Could they be finished already? One entire hour? "You are a fine addition, Lucas."

Imelda was smiling. Minna and Orson were smiling. Even Porch smiled.

"Tomorrow," instructed Porch, "the K. 157 andante. And the mimeographed variations. Practice! You, too," Porch said to Minna.

In the coatroom, Lucas locked up his viola. His jacket lay behind the case and he stepped around it carefully, gently picking it up, his hand covering the pocket.

Minna felt she must say something.

"You have," she began. She cleared her throat. "You have a wonderful vibrato."

Dumb, thought Minna with a sinking in her stomach. It was like saying that he had a lovely skin condition. Or both his legs ended nicely below his trousers.

Lucas nodded.

"I got it at music camp," he said solemnly. He looked apologetic, as if it might have been a mild case of measles, or worse, homesickness.

Lucas put on his jacket, then pulled a frog from

the pocket. The frog was quiet and friendly looking.

"I saved him from the biology lab," explained
Lucas. "I'm going to put him in the park pond. It's
warm enough now." He looked at Minna. "Want
to come?"

"Yes," said Minna quickly before he could change
his mind.

Together they picked up their cases, Minna hoist-
ing hers on her hip, Lucas's under his arm. In the
hallway Lucas pushed the wall button, and it wasn't
until the door opened and closed behind them that
Minna realized she was in the elevator. The walls
were gray with things scribbled there. The floor
was littered with gum wrappers. There was a half-
eaten apple in the corner.

The elevator started down, and Minna put out
her hand to steady herself.

Lucas looked closely at her.

"Elevators can be scary," he said in a soft
voice.

There was a terrible feeling in Minna's chest. The
elevator seemed to drop too fast. There was a loud
whooshing sound in her ears, and she looked at
Lucas to see if he had heard it, too. But he was
smiling at his frog. It was then that Minna knew
about the sinking feeling and the noise in her head.
It was not the elevator.

The door opened at the ground floor.

TV ANNOUNCER: *"After three days and two nights, listeners in the vast audience, Melinda Booth Pratt is about to emerge from her elevator an accomplished cellist. With a vibrato. Accompanying her is Lucas Ellerby. Food and drink have been lowered to them, along with cello music. And flies for their frog."*

Outside there was a slight breeze. McGrew and Emily were still sitting on the stone steps.

"This is Lucas," said Minna. "My brother, McGrew, and his friend Emily Parmalee, a catcher."

Lucas smiled. McGrew smiled. *All this smiling.* Emily Parmalee turned one earring around and around in her ear thoughtfully.

"We're going to put Lucas's frog in the park pond before the bus comes," said Minna.

Behind them the street musicians were beginning to play: a flute on the far corner, Willie, tall and bearded, by the steps playing Vivaldi in the dusk. Willie was Minna's favorite, playing whatever she wanted on his violin, giving her back her money.

They walk down the street, Minna and Lucas with two instruments and a frog between them, McGrew and Emily Parmalee behind, shuffling their feet. The street is crowded but strangely hushed except for the swish sound of cars passing cars. Lucas says nothing. Minna says nothing. Only McGrew breaks the silence.

"Love," he sings softly in a high thin voice behind Minna.

THREE

Minna Pratt is silent on the bus ride home. Emily Parmalee and McGrew are not silent. They sit behind Minna, making up nonsense songs about the bus passengers.

> *"A lady with a dog with its nose glued on;*
> *The dog turns around and its nose is gone. . . ."*

> *"Red dress, blue dress, a green dress, too.*
> *The driver wears a dress and his name is Lew."*

Minna doesn't watch people or count telephone poles or umbrellas or earrings. She thinks about WA Mozart and high third fingers and the elevator. Mostly she thinks about Lucas, defender of frogs and facts. Lucas with the lovely eye that wanders.

Minna stood outside her mother's room, watch–

ing her write. Her mother wore a white oxford cloth shirt that belonged to Minna's father. The sleeves were rolled up, her brown curly hair wild around her face. The typewriter clacked. Papers littered the floor. The television was on.

"Lance . . . I never meant for anything like this to happen. It started innocently. We went to the library to do research together."

"Library, my foot," said Minna's mother to the television. "You were meeting at the YMCA long before the library." She slapped the eraser cartridge into the typewriter.

By her mother's feet there were laundry baskets, one piled on top of another, clothes pouring out, one basket filled to the brim with striped soccer socks. "One red stripe," Minna had once heard her mother complain, "one red stripe with a blue stripe, one red stripe with a green, one blue, one blue and green, one tan, one black with a narrow tan, one tan with a narrow black!" Minna sighed, remembering her father saying that her mother was such a bad housekeeper that they were all in danger of death due to lint buildup.

It had been clear to Minna at an early age—maybe seven—that her mother was different. She hated to cook, except for toast and hot oatmeal that she enjoyed stirring into a mass of beige lumps. She avoided cleaning. Minna's feet stuck to the kitchen floor sometimes, making sucking noises as she walked. You could eat off Emily Parmalee's mother's floor next door. Emily Parmalee once did. But all Minna's mother liked to do was write.

Minna once complained to her father about it.

"Mom's in the land of La," her father had said, smiling, brushing lint off his suit. He stepped over a pile of books and papers to peer in the mirror at his tie.

"The land of La?"

Minna's father was a psychologist. She had read some of his psychology books and thought he should be using words like "obsessive" and "deviant." But her father didn't use these words. Orson Babbitt would use these words, but Minna's father didn't.

"The land of La," he said.

Minna saw his smile. She watched the way he looked at her mother. And Minna came to realize that her father didn't care that her mother was in the land of La. The fact was, he *liked* her there.

Minna sat on the chair by her mother's desk waiting for her to stop typing and begin to ask insane questions. Other mothers asked, "How was your day? Did you pass your math test? What did you have for lunch?" Not Minna's mother. Minna's mother peered into Minna's eyes and asked such questions as, "Do you ever think of love?" Minna longed for her mother to ask something normal, but it rarely happened. "What is the quality of beauty? Of truth?" she would ask, her pencil poised. "Have you ever been in love with an older man?"

Today Minna waited patiently as her mother typed and muttered. At that moment she wished more than anything in the world for her mother to turn around and ask, "Did you fall in love today?" Today Minna could tell her. Minna waited. She looked over her mother's head, reading the letters pinned on her bulletin board. Letters from her readers.

Dear Miss Pratt,
    There is a mispeled word on page 14 of *Marvelous Martha*. I did not love the book.
                                Your fiend,
                                Betsy Brant

Dear Mrs. Pratt,
    My class has to write to a book writer. I wanted to write to Beatrix Potter or Mark Twain but they are dead, so I'm writing to you.
    How are you feeling?
                                Love,
                                Millicent Puff

Dear Mrs. Pratt,
    Hi! Are you married? I'm not.
    You seem very clever in your use of

descriptive words (we call them adverbs and adjectives).

> Regards,
> Butch Reese

Her mother loved the letters and she answered every one. Tacked just below the letters, at eye level when her mother wrote, were her mother's messages. Messages to herself, she called them. They changed often, though one had been there ever since Minna could remember, staring at her every day as if challenging her to understand what it meant.

FACT AND FICTION ARE DIFFERENT TRUTHS

Minna frowned. What did that mean? Facts were true. Wasn't fiction invented? Untrue?

Today there were two new messages.

FICTION IS FACT'S ELDER SISTER—KIPLING

FANCY WITH FACT IS JUST ONE FACT THE
MORE—BROWNING

Minna sighed. She didn't understand those messages either, and she felt a sudden surge of annoyance with her mother for tacking them up. She looked down at her mother's bare feet, watching them tap nervously on the floor as she typed. Her

mother's sneakers lay nearby, one without a shoelace. Minna looked at her own feet, her one sock,
and wondered if what her mother had was catching,
or inherited, like short fingers and low blood sugar.

"Ah! I see you there." Her mother turned off the
electric typewriter and slumped back in her chair,
smiling at Minna.

Ask me. Ask me about love.

"How was chamber group?"

Minna stared. Of all times, a normal question.

"Fine. There's a new violist. A boy," said Minna.
"Lucas."

She waited.

"Lucas?" Her mother leaned on her typewriter.

Ask me.

Her mother wrote the name on a notepad.

"Lucas. A good name," said her mother thoughtfully. She looked at Minna. "Do you ever think
about . . ." she began.

"Yes?" Minna leaned forward eagerly.

"Names," finished her mother. "Do you ever
think about the importance of names?"

Minna stared at the written name. Lucas. She
didn't answer. She knew her mother wasn't really ask-
ing her a question. She was thinking her own thoughts
out loud this time. Answering her own questions.

Seeing the name written on paper was startling,
almost as if Lucas were here in her mother's writing
room, sitting next to Minna. She looked around,

trying to picture him here, sitting in the clutter of her mother's room, surrounded by crumpled papers with bits and pieces of stories written there like coded messages. Minna shrugged her shoulders. It was not to be imagined. Lucas was neat and efficient. He wore two socks, one on each foot, and they matched. He was organized. Organized enough to have a vibrato. Organized enough to have a vibrato *and* to have a frog tucked safely inside his pocket. Was that the answer? Organization? No. There was a time when Minna had been organized. She had written in a journal, keeping track of herself on paper, reading herself from time to time. No, that was not all there was to Lucas's vibrato. That was not all there was to *Lucas*.

Minna's mother began typing again, slowly at first, then gathering speed like a ball rolling down a long hill. Minna sat for a while on the edge of her chair, watching her mother work. Her mother never saw her leave the room.

Dinner is quiet. McGrew hums into his whipped potatoes. Minna's father smiles at Minna's mother and loves her dinner, hamburger wrapped around dill pickles. Soon it will be time for dessert. Then Minna will go upstairs and close the bedroom door behind her. She will practice WA Mozart for the first time in a long time. She will practice and practice until she finds her vibrato, wherever it may be.

FOUR

The telephone call comes that evening at eight thirty, just as Minna is finishing her homework. McGrew answers.

"What!" he says into the phone.

Minna grins. She loves the way McGrew answers the phone.

"Hold still," he tells the caller. "It's him," he sings to Minna.

Him. Minna knows who him is, even though it is not the only him who has ever called her.

"Hello."

"Hello," says Lucas. "Which quartet do we have for tomorrow? I can't remember."

"K. 156," says Minna. She smiles because she does not believe that organized Lucas would forget. "And the andante of 157. And don't forget the Don-izetti variations . . . Lucas," she adds because she has not yet called him by his name. She remembers her mother telling her that for the first whole week that Minna was born her mother called her "baby," "it," or "her." When she was home all alone one day her mother leaned over and whispered "Melinda" and burst into tears because it made her baby real.

"What?" asks Minna. "What did you say?"

"Dinner," repeats Lucas. "We can walk to my house and eat dinner. Someone will bring you home. We could even practice together. Or not," he adds quickly.

Dinner with Lucas. It sounds like a book title. *Dinner with Lucas.*

"Okay," she says.

"Okay," says Lucas.

Then the phone goes dead. Lucas has hung up without saying good-bye. Minna hangs up and the phone rings again.

"Hello?"

"Good-bye," says Lucas.

The bus was filled with sunlight and noise. Minna sat next to the window, McGrew and Emily Parmalee in the front seat swapping stories with their favorite bus driver, Lewis. Lewis was a stout pleasant man who had eight stout children who were also pleasant, and another on the way. Minna couldn't imagine having so many children in one house. She pictured them bouncing off the floors to the walls and up to the ceilings and back again like a hot panful of popping corn. Lewis had brought some of them on the bus from time to time. They had non-stout names, like Rilla and Wesley and Blythe.

Minna took out her school notebook and underlined her vocabulary words: <u>imaginary</u>, <u>listless</u>, <u>et cetera</u>, <u>vegetarian</u>. She wrinkled her forehead. Her teacher, Miss Barbizon, always made the class write short stories using the words. It was, Minna thought, a very bad idea. The stories were also very bad. "Every story must have a beginning, a middle, and an end, remember," Miss Barbizon would say with bright surprised eyes, as if the idea had just occurred to her.

Minna took out her pencil and licked the point because it made her write better. She wrote:

> My bus driver friend, Lewis, drives a bus that is not <u>imaginary</u>. Lewis is not imaginary either, and he is not at all <u>listless</u>. What Lewis is is a <u>vegetarian</u>. This means he does not eat cows and sheep, turtles or toads. <u>Et cetera</u>.
>
> The end.

Minna smiled. A beginning, a middle, and an end. Miss Barbizon would like it. The class would like it. Et cetera.

Outside the bus Minna stood for a moment on the street, shading her eyes. McGrew and Emily Parmalee climbed down the bus steps behind her.

"We're going to a movie," said Emily. "A foreign film. McGrew likes to sing the subtitles."

Minna watched them walk down the street, picturing them fifty years from now doing exactly the same thing: McGrew with gray whiskers, humming, Emily Parmalee, her pockets loaded with jujubes for the movies, great whopper earrings hanging from her ears.

The sound of Mozart came from down the block—Willie on the street corner. The bus started up, sending warm puffs of exhaust after her. Minna picked up her cello and walked to where a group of listeners stood. Someone in the front row tossed money in the open violin case. A small brown dog sidled up, sniffed the case, then lay down and gazed up at Willie. Willie finished and the crowd applauded and slowly, reluctantly, moved off. He smiled at Minna and took a red handkerchief from his pocket to wipe the rosin off his instrument. He wore a matching handkerchief tied around his neck and a dark blue shirt with a button missing; the shoelaces on his boots did not match. Minna thought suddenly of her mother's missing shoelace.

She took a quarter out of her pocket and handed it to Willie.

"Thank you for playing," she said.

Willie bowed.

"You're welcome." He gave her back the quarter. "And I thank *you* for listening."

Minna grinned. It was their ritual, as reassuring as the sounds of her father snoring at night, McGrew's humming, the savage clash of pans in the kitchen when her mother began breakfast. Willie was always there when Minna went to the conservatory, standing on the same corner, like the gargoyles, playing music she loved. They never talked about anything else . . . only music. Sometimes they hardly spoke at all.

Minna left Willie and Mozart and the small brown dog in the sun and climbed the conservatory steps. Small children pushed past her, carrying small cases. She could hear a Suzuki class on the first floor, dozens of fiddlers playing variations of "Twinkle Twinkle" together. She could picture them in foot-long skirts or jeans with reinforced knees, with cigar-box-size violins, all standing. She remembered her own quarter-size cello stored somewhere in the attic, a small piece of Minna's past.

Minna pushed open the door to the rehearsal room and Lucas was there, just as Minna had remembered him. He waved to her.

Orson opened his music folder.

"Ode to Joy!" he exclaimed, peering at the sheet

of music on his stand. "Blah. A lackluster piece. New word, lackluster," he explained to Porch. "Dull and lacking in radiance. Why can't we play the entire Ninth Symphony?"

Porch smiled wryly.

"You're good, Orson, but you are not a symphony. And if you play it well you will not find it a lackluster piece."

"Anything worth doing is worth doing well," quoted Imelda.

Minna unzipped her cello case and took out her cello and bow.

"Speaking of doing things well," said Porch, his hands behind his back, "did you practice, Orson?"

"I always practice," said Orson brightly.

"Without your bow?" Porch held Orson's bow in his hands.

There was a silence. Lucas crossed his feet, smiling faintly. Minna stood still, her cello leaning against her.

"I plucked," said Orson.

"A canny boy," said Porch. He handed Orson his bow and looked at them. "*That* means shrewd. Now we shall all be shrewd," said Porch sternly.

Orson sat, a broad grin on his face, his hair wild as if a wren had flown in it and out again.

"Legato, remember," Porch said, raising his violin. "One note connecting to another; smooth and big and"—he smiled at them—"full of radiance."

Minna looks sideways at Lucas, who knows she is looking at him. He smiles at his music, his head bent, his hand placed firmly in place on the strings. His hair falls down over his forehead and Minna thinks about radiance. A good word. Minna feels full of radiance. Maybe it's the music that makes her feel that way, *Ode to Joy*, after all. Maybe it's Lucas's vibrato. Maybe. Maybe not.

FIVE

"*E*levator or stairs?" asked Lucas in the hall-way.

Minna wanted to choose the stairs, but after a moment she reached out and pressed the elevator button. Inside she held her cello with one hand, grasping the handrail with the other so tightly that her knuckles turned white. The elevator bumped and began to move. There was no litter today. The wrappers and apple cores and empty soda cans had been removed. Minna read what had been written on the walls. MARSHA EATS GRASS. MARIO IS AN ICON-OCLAST.

"What does that mean, iconoclast?" asked Minna. Lucas shook his head.

"I don't know," he said. He smiled at her. "We'll look it up."

Minna thought suddenly about her mother's messages tacked up on her wall for her to read but

31

not understand. Could she look them up some-where?

The door opened at the second floor and a herd of small children crowded in, arguing about sharps and flats.

"Is so," hissed a girl with only a scattering of teeth. "A G-flat *is* the same as an F-sharp."

"Is not!"

"Is so!"

Lucas grinned at Minna over their heads. The elevator door opened and they ran off down the hall.

It was a short walk to Lucas's house, past apart-ment buildings and stores: a book shop with a cat sleeping in the window, curled around a thesaurus; another window filled with china and glass. Street vendors sold hot dogs and roasted walnuts from pushcarts, buses and cars streamed by them, a woman pushed a stroller with a sleeping child, a balloon tied to his wrist. They passed a pet store.

"Sometimes I buy frogs here," said Lucas.

They stopped to peer in. Gerbils slept in shredded newspaper, a parrot sitting on a perch opened its bill at them.

Minna counted twelve trees growing along the streets with twelve black cast-iron fences around them. Two children played hopscotch on the street, the outlines neatly chalked in white. They played with flat stones, and they were very serious. Lucas stopped to watch.

"I've never played hopscotch," he said.

Minna looked at him.

"Never ever?"

Lucas shook his head. "I don't have any brothers or sisters, you know."

"But your parents could teach you," said Minna. She had, until this moment, forgotten that it was her mother who had taught her. It had been a hot windless day, and her mother had drawn hopscotch squares on the sidewalk outside and been fierce about winning. Minna smiled at the memory.

"My parents are not the hopscotch type," said Lucas beside her.

"What about kick the can?"

"No."

Minna pushed her hair back behind her ears.

"Well, I'll teach you then," she said matter-of-factly, making Lucas smile.

They walked past a tall brick building with white pillars.

"This is where I go to school," said Lucas. "The Academy." He lowered his voice and intoned solemnly, "The Academy." Minna laughed.

They passed a fire station with two great yellow trucks inside, a chair set by the door, waiting for a fireman to sit there in the spring sunlight.

"Will you go to music camp again this summer?" asked Minna.

"Yes," said Lucas thoughtfully. "Or no. My parents want me to."

Minna smiled.

"So you are the no. Right?"

"Yes and no," said Lucas. He stopped. "Here we are."

Minna stands very still, staring. She does not even hear the street traffic, the conversation of the passersby. The house where Lucas lives is tall and brick, like the school, with a courtyard and trees in front. There are white shutters on the windows and window boxes. On the door hangs a shining door knocker, shaped like a dragon.

"Home," says Lucas with a shrug.

Speechless, Minna follows Lucas up the walk. She knows the house will be clean. It is. The entry room, nearly as large as the conservatory rehearsal room, is tiled and so shiny that Minna thinks it is wet. A winding stairway goes up and up, large paintings of grim well-dressed people lining the walls. There are many rooms with high ceilings, with groups of furniture here and there. In the living room there is a great fireplace. No one fills the gleaming space. It is like a wonderful barn Minna had once seen, empty of cows.

"Home," repeated Lucas, falling into a chair.

"Quiet," said Minna, looking around. "And big

enough," she added, "for us to play kick the can."

Lucas burst out laughing. Then he peered at Minna. "If you died," he said, suddenly serious, his voice loud, "what would you want to come back to life as?"

Minna frowned. Was this a test? It sounded like a question her mother would ask, and she did not want her mother intruding in this peaceful place. But it was Lucas who had asked the question. She could tell him that she hadn't thought about it, but that would be a lie. She had thought about it often. She was just too embarrassed to tell Lucas that what she wanted to be in her next life was a ferret. She had seen a ferret once on the street, a tiny red collar around its neck, being led on a leash. It was gray-brown with sharp wise eyes and tiny feet, and it was friendly. It was also content. It didn't need a vibrato.

Lucas leaned forward, waiting.

"McGrew . . ." began Minna slowly, "McGrew wants to be a flying squirrel. Or a slug. Slugs drink through their skin, you know."

Lucas smiled broadly. "Does Imelda know that fact?"

Minna smiled back at him. There was a silence. Minna stared at her feet, then at the border patterns that twisted and turned on the oriental rug.

"Come on," said Lucas finally with a sigh. He stood up and pulled Minna to her feet. "I'll show you what *I* want to be."

Minna followed Lucas up the winding stairway, twenty-two steps to the second-floor landing. Lucas started up a second flight, but Minna stopped, staring at a room with glass and plants and white wicker furniture. It was filled with light.

"That's my mother's solarium," said Lucas from above. "It's where she spends a lot of time, thinking up dinner conversation topics. Come up!"

Minna turned and walked up twenty-two steps to the third floor. Lucas opened a door and beckoned to her.

It was Lucas's room, Minna could tell. There were boxes and books, a music stand in the corner, a stack of music on a shelf. A small violin leaned in the far corner, left over from a time when Lucas was little. A bit of Lucas's history, *his* past. And then Minna saw the glass tanks, at least a half dozen of them lined up along one wall, all filled with frogs. There were small frogs, large frogs, some jumping in the water, some sitting on rocks and mossy places. One tank was filled with water and tadpoles.

"A frog," said Minna, smiling. "You want to come back as a frog." She thought of the first time she had seen Lucas, the frog he had saved from biology lab hidden in his pocket.

Lucas nodded.

"See," he said softly. "You didn't laugh."

"No," said Minna.

"You know what I'd really like to be someday?" Lucas went on before Minna could speak. "A biologist, or a naturalist."

"Not a musician?" asked Minna, surprised. "Not a violist?"

"No." He turned his head to look at her. "I've never told anyone this before. Never ever. My parents don't even know about the frogs."

"Why not?" whispered Minna.

Lucas shrugged his shoulders. "They never come up here. They say that children need room and space to grow in. Room and space of their own."

"Well," said Minna, "there is space for all of us to grow here."

She walked to the windows. *Lucas's world here. His all alone. My parents spill out and tumble all over my house.* She turned.

"But you play so well."

"So do you," said Lucas. "Do you want to be a professional musician?"

Minna was silent. For a moment she thought mean thoughts. Traitorous thoughts. *What a waste of a vibrato.* Or was it? Her father had once told Minna that nothing was a waste. She doubted it. She looked out the window over the buildings across the street, to the park and the pond where they had walked to free Lucas's frog. She could see the peaked roof of the conservatory in the distance, the familiar gargoyles lurking underneath the eaves. It was like living above the world here, looking down at everything in its proper place; the "eternal fitness of things," her father called it. For the first time in Minna's life she knew what he meant.

She took a deep breath.

"Lucas?"

"What?"

"I want to be a ferret."

She turned around just in time to see his smile.

There was a silence, the only sounds in the room the splashes of frogs in the water, a steady hum of the fish tank. At last Lucas took her hand.

"Come on," he said.

Lucas pulled her out the door, down the forty-four steps not counting the landings, past the solarium, through the entry way, and through double-swinging doors with brass edges into the kitchen. The room was huge and clean and white. A girl stood at the sink washing lettuce. She was dressed all in white with white stockings and shoes, like a nurse.

"Twig," said Lucas, breathless, still holding Minna's hand. "This is Minna."

The girl looked at Minna. She turned off the water and shook the lettuce in the sink.

"You can tell Twig," said Lucas.

Minna, confused, looked at Lucas.

"You mean about being a ferret?" she asked.

"Ah," said Twig thoughtfully, "a good choice,

ferret. I myself devoutly wish to be a penguin."

A penguin, a ferret, a frog. Minna was seized by verse.

> *A penguin, a ferret, a frog, tra-la,*
> *Sing sweet happy songs in a bog, tra-la.*

Minna stared at Twig, who looked less like a penguin than anyone Minna had ever seen. She was tall and thin with pale straight hair and large eyes. She looked more like a fish on its feet than a penguin.

"Twig is our housekeeper," said Lucas.

"A housekeeper? I've never known a housekeeper," said Minna.

Twig moved silently about the kitchen from refrigerator to countertop to sink.

"And now you do," she said in a soft voice.

"Your new soft-soled shoes really work," said Lucas admiringly.

Twig nodded.

"Quiet, you know. To sneak up on thieves and killers and kids," she confided to Minna. She waved her hand. "And other lowlifes as well. You never know who or what will hover about." Twig pronounced the word "hoover." Minna smiled.

"Twig could sneak up on a cockroach," said Lucas.

"Twig has," said Twig ominously, disappearing into the dark cave of a dining room with some dishes. "But," she stuck her head back in the kitchen, "don't tell your Mum and Dad."

Lucas gave Minna a level look.

"And that is Twig," he said.

And that is Twig. Minna walked to the dining room door and opened it with one finger, peering in. *Just what I need. Another wish. I wish I had a vibrato.* Minna sighed. *Now I wish I had a Twig.*

Lucas's parents arrive late and are very polite. They are short with high foreheads, and though they do not look like Lucas, they look very much like each other. They speak, thinks Minna, in the manner of kings and queens.

"Am I to presume you are Melinda Pratt?" asks Mr. Ellerby, shaking her hand.

"Yes," says Minna.

"Delightful," pronounces Mrs. Ellerby. "And you are a cellist?"

Minna smiles. She likes that. She has never before thought of herself as a "cellist"; until this moment she has only played the cello.

"We are honored to have you here," says Mr. Ellerby. "You must plan to come again."

Minna loves their talk; she is hypnotized by it.

Dinner is chicken by candlelight and good china with no chips. Over dinner the Ellerbys' conversation changes; it becomes soft and legato, like music; like a small quiet stream with no rocks. Little punctuation, no outbursts.

The street will be repaved soon, dear, says Mrs. Ellerby.

Is that so? says Mr. Ellerby.

The price of eggs, I hear, is up, says Mrs. Ellerby.

Oil, too, says Mr. Ellerby.

Twig drifts in and out of the room on her soft-soled shoes, creeping up on conversation, sneaking in on thoughts. Minna cannot stop looking at her.

You will be fine musicians someday, Melinda and Lucas, pronounces Mrs. Ellerby.

Lucas's foot touches Minna's under the table.

That is so, says Mr. Ellerby, without looking up from his braised chicken.

Lucas grins across the table at Minna, and Minna smiles into her plate.

Maybe, maybe no, thinks Minna. *You are quiet and polite and clean people, Mrs. Ellerby, Mr. Ellerby. You know lots about the price of eggs and oil. Your conversation is splendid and organized. But there is something you don't know. I know it, though. Lucas knows it.*

Minna looks up as Twig slips her plate away, one entire congealed serving of cold creamed onions still there, hidden by a lettuce leaf. She winks at Minna.

Twig knows it too, Mr. and Mrs. Ellerby. Maybe we'll be fine musicians one day. But there is more.

I will be a ferret. Your son will be a frog.

And that *is so. Tra-la.*

SIX

For the first time in Minna's life she is on time for something. It is not a mistake. Minna has planned it, an early cello lesson before chamber group. She has wakened at dawn, even though it is a Saturday, in order to begin plans for the rest of her life on a sheet of notepaper. Minna's early life has been strung out in ordered sentences on paper, like an outline for her life.

> MINNA, AGE 7: *Ware plad skirt to school.*
> *Punch Richard.*
> MINNA, AGE 8: *Do not forgit spelling list.*
> MINNA, AGE 10: *Plan to be a movie star.*
> *Learn to faint.*
> MINNA, AGE 11: *Living by the sea is preferable.*

Minna stopped planning her life all of a sudden. Now it is time to plan again. Minna sits on her bed with a blank sheet of paper. Thoughts of Lucas's peaceful clean house fill her mind: quiet dinners, soft lights, polite and kind parents, murmurs. And Twig, like an orchestra conductor, leading them all calmly through a symphony dinner, from beginning to end without mistakes, without interruption, without clutter. "Is there anything you wish?" Lucas's mother asks her. "Anything at all?" After dinner, each person goes to his place: Mr. Ellerby in his study, Mrs. Ellerby in her solarium, Lucas in his third-floor room by the attic door. Boundaries, thinks Minna. There are boundaries there. Minna sighs and leans back on her pillows to dream a dream without sleeping. She is the only musician in an orchestra. It is a solo symphony, but there are many conductors: Twig in soft-soled shoes, her mother directing with an eraser cartridge, her father smiling and waving his glasses, Porch frowning. "Play," they whisper to her, "play." When her daydream ends it is too late to plan her life. She hears her mother crashing about the typewriter. The blank sheet of paper remains empty.

Minna rode the bus alone, leaving Emily Parmalee and McGrew at home surrounded by books and papers as they worked on their science reports. Emily was writing on the decline of maple trees. Emily had always been interested in trees. McGrew's report was titled "The How and Why of the Beaver."

The streets were grimy with spring. Willie played Tchaikovsky on the corner, music that made Minna feel sad and peaceful at the same time. Next to the violin case the small brown dog slept, curled like a sausage on Willie's jacket. A woman in a fur coat with worn elbows stood in front of Minna, a baby peering over her shoulder, his head bobbing as he stared at Minna. The baby grinned suddenly and drooled down his mother's back, leaving a wet trail of fur where his mother couldn't see. A slimy secret between Minna and the baby. Minna touched his hand and moved off through the crowd, standing on the steps for a moment, watching Willie. She sighed and looked up at the gargoyles. *Willie on the street corner has a vibrato. Where is mine?*

Inside it was dark and quiet and cool. Porch beckoned Minna in and unzipped her cello case. Minna slumped in a chair.

"Min?" asked Porch. He sat down next to her. "Problems?"

"It's my vibrato," said Minna, looking at him.

"What about it?"

"Where is it?" Minna's voice was loud in the empty room. "I mean," she leaned forward, "Lucas has a vibrato. Even Willie has one. Where is mine?"

Porch frowned at Minna.

"William Gray?" he said sharply. "What do you mean 'even' Willie? What do you know about Willie?"

Minna's face reddened. She had not even known Willie's full name.

"Nothing, except that he's always there, playing on the street corner. He always gives me my money back," she added softly.

Porch's face softened.

"He does, does he? A gift. Willie is a fine musician, Minna. And he was a fine musician before he got his vibrato. Did you know he plays in the symphony chamber group?"

"But why does he play on the street?" asked Minna, surprised.

"For his own reasons, Minna," said Porch. "You might ask him that yourself."

"We never talk about anything but music," said Minna.

"Well," said Porch, sitting down and leaning back in his chair, "life and music are not separate, you know."

There was a silence.

"Min," said Porch, "your vibrato is not something that is there, I mean that exists, like fingernails, or hair about to grow longer. It is something you can work at, yes, and think about, yes, but it is much more like . . ." Porch folded his arms, "like understanding something for the first time, or suddenly knowing what a book you're reading is all about." He peered at Minna. "It is like a light going on over your head. Do you know what I mean?"

"No," said Minna, staring at Porch. She was thinking about her past life; the moments along the way when she needed something to make things right. When she was seven it had been a plaid skirt, at ten it had been a bicycle. Then it had been her first full-size cello. Now it was a vibrato. Would it end there?

"You will understand," said Porch. "You will." He tapped her knee. "Ready for Mozart?"

Minna sat up, gripping her cello by its neck. She stared at the music, thinking about Willie and her mother and father. Did she know them at all, even the slightest little bit?

"I'll never be ready for Mozart," said Minna.

"Ah," said Porch, "but Mozart is ready for you, Minna Pratt. Come on, let's do K. 158. Your favorite key."

Minna couldn't help smiling. Porch was right, it was her favorite key. Sometimes, *most* of the time, Porch knew Minna as well as anyone else did. Except for McGrew; McGrew who knew, for instance, that in spite of Minna's grumbling, in spite of her complaints, Minna played the cello because she wanted to.

Porch picked up his violin.

"Let's play the repeats," said Porch. He turned to look at Minna. "And we will play it wonderfully. In tune. With or without a vibrato."

And they did.

"Hey!"

Porch and Minna looked up, startled. Imelda stood in the doorway. She pointed to Minna.

"*She's* here. Am I late?"

"Don't worry about it," said Porch. "Just come in and tune."

Orson skidded in behind Imelda, Lucas behind him. Minna could tell that Lucas had frogs in his pockets, just by the way he took off his jacket. He held up two fingers. Two fingers, two frogs. He smiled slyly at her.

"The whole caboodle," commented Orson. "That means the whole pack of us," he told Minna. He unlocked his case and took out his violin, running his fingers up and down the strings to make wailing sounds.

"Do you know," said Imelda, "that Mozart once fainted because of a horrible noise? It's a fact."

Porch sighed.

"I can believe it," he said. "Let's get to it. Music, that is." He raised his bow. "The whole caboodle."

After scales they begin the Mozart, the dreaded one that Minna does and does not love. The allegro goes well, but the andante looms and Minna frowns as she waits. She has eleven measures of rests, the longest time in the world, the mournful, wonderful eleven measures as the violins and viola wind about each other. She lifts her bow and slips in, pianissimo, fine for a while until she comes to the sixteenth notes that are hers. Hers all alone. She can hear that her fingers are not stretching, not reaching. Porch nods at her encouragingly. "Repeat now," he says, and she bites her lip and repeats, trying to force her fingers to obey. Better. The repeat is better. Nearly in tune. Is there such a thing as *nearly* in tune? At last there is the coda, peaceful and solid. And then, with sudden wildness they fall into the presto, Orson bowing so vigorously that the bow shoots from his hand, retrieved by Lucas, handed back with laughter. Imelda sits primly and makes soft mistakes. Lucas plays calmly, eyeing his jacket on the floor. It moves a bit, two frogs in the pocket. Minna plays in tune. No vibrato. She looks up quickly. No light over her head.

"Grand," said Porch, leaning back in his chair, his legs stretched out in front of him. "Quite grand, in fact. Minna, much better, that difficult part." He spoke a musical code. "Press hard, those fingers, left hand." He looked at Orson. "I do think that the presto was a bit too presto." Orson smiled.

"Now," said Porch. "I have an announcement." Everyone looked up.

"There is a competition eight weeks from now.

Eight, a long time." He stood up and folded his arms across his chest. "For the first time this composition includes musicians of your age. About ten quartets will perform. Less experienced fiddlers."

That's us, thought Minna with a cold flash of fear. Less experienced.

"And," said Porch with a smile, "I think you are ready. I *know* you are ready."

Even me with no vibrato?

"I don't know," said Orson in an uncertain voice.

Imelda frowned. Lucas leaned over to hang his bow from the music stand. It swayed a bit, then stopped.

"There is," said Porch, "an added incentive besides beautiful music. A prize of one hundred dollars each, if you win, to be used, we all hope, to further your musical careers." Minna looked quickly at Lucas. Not Lucas, she thought. Lucas would buy glass aquariums. Dead flies. Do frogs eat *dead* flies?

"Well," said Porch, "what do you think?"

Silence. Minna wanted to shout "No!"

"It is," said Porch, "a wonderful experience. Not winning," he added, "playing."

More silence, except for Imelda's foot tapping nervously on the floor.

"Could we use the money for something else?" asked Imelda suddenly, her foot tapping faster. Orson's music slipped off his stand.

Books of facts for Imelda, thought Minna.

"Anything at all!" Porch exclaimed. "Does that

mean yes?" His eyebrows raised, he looked at them. He smiled then and leaned down to pick up Orson's music. And looking pleased, he made the decision. The decision that made Minna's skin prickle.

"We'll play the Mozart," he said softly.

Silently they picked up their music, packed up their instruments, and filed out. They were in the elevator, riding down, before Minna realized where she was. She shivered even though the elevator was warm.

"Maybe I'd buy a new bow," said Orson. Minna was suddenly aware they had been talking about the competition, about the prize money.

A new bow? Orson, who gags through all chamber music?

"A good permanent, extra curly," announced Imelda as the elevator jolted to a stop.

Imelda with her wonderful shiny-smooth hair? Who are these people?

They walked outside, blinking in the light. Willie was tuning. Money clinked into his open case. The dog was there looking wise and knowing, like a music critic.

Minna stopped on the steps. Lucas put his hand on her arm.

"What would you buy with the money?" he asked.

Minna shook her head. She thought about plaid skirts and bicycles and cellos. And vibratos. But you couldn't buy a vibrato.

"I wish," she began. "I wish I didn't have to tell my mother and father about this. I won't tell them. They'll just make a big fuss."

Lucas smiled.

"That's nice, a fuss. My parents have never come to hear me play a recital."

"*That's* nice," said Minna. "They leave you alone."

"Yes," said Lucas so softly that Minna almost didn't hear. He bent down to pat the dog.

Willie tucked his violin under his chin.

"What's your pleasure?" he called to them. "Happy or sad?"

"Willie?" said Minna.

"Yes?" The violin dipped a little as he looked at her.

"What would you do with one hundred dollars?"

Willie looked surprised.

"A question about something other than music?" he asked, smiling.

Lucas stirred beside her.

"Or two hundred," he added.

"Two hundred dollars?" Willie tucked his violin under one arm. "That's easy. I'd go visit Mama. Back home. She likes to sit on the porch and hear me play. She says it makes her garden grow." Willie tuned his violin and peered at them. "And you know what? It does."

Minna had never thought of a mama for Willie before. But of course everyone had one at one time or another, a mama. *She* had one.

Is that why he plays on the street corner? Getting home to Mama? Minna peered up at Willie. How old was he? It was hard to tell. He had curly hair and was tall. He didn't have any wrinkles or gray hair, so he must be younger than her parents, who were beginning to develop both. Did he live nearby? Did he have brothers or sisters? She closed her eyes as he tuned. She didn't even know what he thought about. She wondered if he ever thought of . . . Minna's eyes blew open. Just like my mother, she thought, shocked. I am thinking just like my mother. It *is* catching!

"Happy music or sad?" repeated Willie.

Willie played a few notes, wandering across the strings. Lucas pulled on Minna's sleeve, gesturing to his pocket. The frogs. Minna had forgotten.

"Happy," she told Willie. "Happy!" she called, walking backward as Lucas pulled her toward the pond. Someone stopped to pat the brown dog. Minna and Lucas waved good-bye to Willie, who raised his eyebrows good-bye back to them. And then he lifted his bow with a great flourish and played an arpeggio so bright that it seemed to call out the sun to follow them down the street and away.

SEVEN

Spring appears violently, rain and sun and rain again. The earth is muddy and Minna's mother, wearing heels, sinks into the front lawn as she walks to the car. Minna practices. She practices on and on. She practices so much, so often, that her mother stops writing to listen. Her father comes out of his study to stand at her door. He carries a textbook on adolescent behavior. McGrew hums and smiles and begins spring baseball.

Minna's mother had gone to the dentist. Minna walked into her mother's writing room. Her mother had begun to clean but had stopped midway, leaving behind a strange combination of chaos and order. In the typewriter was a page, a page numbered 1 with two typed sentences, double spaced. It was, Minna knew, a book beginning. She sat down and read.

Leila fell in love at noon. The boy was tall and slim and distracted.

Minna frowned. "Distracted." Did that mean grand looking and nearly perfectly organized? With a vibrato? With corn-colored hair?

Minna looked it up in the dictionary.

Distraction: 1. A distracting, or state of being distracted; perplexity, confusion, disorder.

Not Lucas, thought Minna. Her mother, maybe, but not Lucas.

2. Agitation from violent emotions; hence, mental derangement; madness.

Her mother. Definitely her mother. Minna leaned back and read the signs above her mother's desk. The old ones were there, the confusing ones. Minna leaned forward. There were two new ones.

THE WRITER WRITES ABOUT THE WRITER

ALL SERIOUS DARING COMES FROM WITHIN
—EUDORA WELTY

The writer. Her mother? Minna read the two new sentences in her mother's typewriter again. She thought of her mother falling in love at noon. She closed her eyes, trying to picture the scene, her mother young, in shorts and braids, falling in love in the midday heat. Her father, sweating, leaning on his bicycle, both of them confused and perplexed. As hard as Minna tried, all she could see was her mother's room, half clean, her father in a suit, tripping over books, all of them, the lot, in danger of falling into distraction. Minna sighed, opening her eyes. There, almost magically, as if she were seeing clearly for the first time, were two matching red-striped socks, hanging over the side of the clothes basket. She gathered them up, rolling them into a tight neat ball.

"Are my glasses here?"

Minna's father stood in the doorway.

"What are you doing?" he asked.

"Sorting socks," said Minna, looking around for his glasses. His glasses were "eternally lost," as her mother put it. McGrew had once drawn a picture of their father looking for them, a line drawing of a man with a candle in the night, bare feet, a nightshirt, and a lost expression.

"Sorting socks to keep from becoming distracted," Minna added.

Her father bent over the clothes basket and came up with a black case. He grinned at her.

"Ah, distraction," said her father, putting on his glasses. They were half glasses, ones he could look over or through at her. "You mean like messy rooms? And lost glasses?"

"Is it a disease?" asked Minna.

"No," said her father, putting his arm around her, "it's a condition. More like freckles or night blindness."

"Not fatal," said Minna.

"Not fatal," he echoed.

"I'll tell you something about distraction," said her father, smiling. "Once, just before I asked your mother to marry me, I opened her closet door and looked inside."

"And?" asked Minna.

"And," said her father, "it was like a look into the future. A hint of things to come."

"That bad," said Minna, smiling.

"I closed the door again," he said.

"Papa?"

"What?"

"Did you fall in love at noon?"

"At noon," said her father promptly, "and every day thereafter at 3:00, and at 5:30 and again at 6:45, 11:10, and 4:22, and at . . ."

"Minna?" McGrew poked his head in the doorway. "Baseball practice today. And Emily Parmalee's got her feathers," he sang. "Want to come?"

Minna looked up at her father. He shook his head and, having found his glasses, went off to his books and his patients. Minna closed the door of her mother's writing room and left. Away from distractions and closets and laundry baskets and love at all hours. She went off with those she could count on, McGrew and Emily Parmalee. Off to the spring mud.

Minna sits in the grandstands. They are not really grandstands; they are three tiers of bleacher seats, scattered with parents and brothers and sisters watching practice. Her parents should be here, but they aren't. McGrew waves to Minna from left field. He likes left field because he can hum without interruption. Emily Parmalee is behind the plate, hunkered down in her uniform and face mask and cleats. Minna sighs and thinks about facts. Baseball is simple. There are facts there. You either know them or not. Hit. Bunt. Run. Slide. Baseball is not like love, which is confusing. It is not like Mozart, which Minna cannot play the same way twice and never perfectly. Baseball is not like her mother's messages above her typewriter, which Minna does not understand.

Minna watches Emily Parmalee. Her uniform is dirty, the bill of her baseball cap turned up. But as Minna leans forward to look more closely, she can see, just below Emily Parmalee's cap, two more facts. Nearly hidden by the face mask and next to a dirt smudge are bright pink feather earrings.

EIGHT

Minna, McGrew, and Emily Parmalee walked home after practice, McGrew singing the national anthem one beat off:

"Oh . . . oh . . . oh say can you
See by the dawn's early
Light what so proudly we
Hailed at the twilight's last gleam . . ."

Their team, the Moles, had played well, with Emily making a final dramatic out at home plate. McGrew, lost in thought, had dropped the one fly ball that came to him.

"I was thinking about my science report," he explained to Emily.

"Didn't you wonder what all the shouting was about?" asked Emily kindly.

"No," said McGrew. "I didn't hear the shouting."

"Did the sunlight get in your eyes?" asked Minna.

"There isn't any bright sunlight," he pointed out. *Honest McGrew*.

"Dad should teach you how to catch a ball the right way," said Minna. "He should!"

"Yes," said McGrew. "But I don't know if Dad can do it."

Minna looked sharply at him, suddenly thinking of Lucas's words: *My parents are not the hopscotch type.*

Minna put the end of the middle finger of her left hand in the palm of her right, moving it back and forth absentmindedly.

"What are you doing?" asked Emily Parmalee. She took off her catcher's mask and her feathered earrings blew back like beagles' ears in the wind.

"I'm practicing my vibrato. I have a lesson this afternoon."

"Vibrato? Is it a trick?" asked Emily.

"Yes," said McGrew. "Vibrato," he recited, "is a tremulous or pulsating effect for adding warmth and beauty to the tone in music."

Minna smiled. McGrew sounded like Imelda.

"It makes the music sound better," he sang, shaking his head to show the vibrato effect.

Emily nodded thoughtfully.

"A trick," she agreed.

Minna sighed.

"Lucas has a wonderful vibrato, Orson's on his way. Imelda soon. I want one," said Minna, still practicing in her hand.

Emily shrugged. "Some people can do things that others can't." She looked at McGrew. "*I* can catch," she said wisely.

"True," sang McGrew.

They walk up the sidewalk to Minna's house, past a rake lying in soggy leaves left over from last fall; past brown, crisp flowers in pots that Minna's mother forgot to bring in for the winter; past three huge green trash bags sitting on the porch, something oozing from one. Minna thinks about Lucas's neat brick pathway through his neat brick courtyard. They walk through the kitchen, where there is a saucepan with last night's baked beans crusting over, a sink full of dirty dishes. Spilled sugar crunches under their feet. There is a note on the dining room table next to two dirty coffee cups, a pile of underwear, and the morning mail.

Gone shopping,

Ma

Beside the note is a letter from one of their mother's readers. It is typewritten with many x's and a curious pattern of capital and lowercase letters.

> DEar Mrxxs. PRatt,
>
> I have TWo questions that only you, a WRiter, can ansxxswer because I know that writerxs know the anSwers.
>
> 1. HOw much does a tripewriter cost?
> 2. How do moths FLY?
>
> > Love,
> > Kiki

Minna stared at the letter. She knew her mother would spend a long time thinking about her answer. She would call typewriter stores to ask for information.

"The moth question will take Mama days of research," said McGrew, as if he had read Minna's thoughts.

"How come?" asked Emily Parmalee. "All moths do is move their wings. Up and down, you know?"

Minna and McGrew laughed, but Minna's throat felt tight. There was a sour restless feeling in her stomach. She left Emily and McGrew arguing quietly about moth wings and fly balls and wandered into her mother's writing room.

I have, thought Minna closing her eyes, memorized the mess. Just as Mozart, so Imelda had informed them just this week, could identify chords and tones blindfolded when he was a child. Maybe

I will be one of Imelda's facts someday, thought Minna: *The Lone Cellist Left in the World Without a Vibrato*. She moved around boxes of books and papers until she bumped against her mother's typing table. She thought of Lucas's house, where she could, if she wished, dance wildly, blindfolded, without bumping against anything. Minna opened her eyes and looked at a sheet of paper in the typewriter.

Dear Kiki,
　　Thank you for your letter . . .

Minna sat down slowly.

　. . . regarding typewriters and moths. I certainly don't have all the answers, but I can tell you that the price of typewriters depends on whether you use manual or electric. Manual, of course, are less expensive and you can often get a second-hand typewriter. Electric cost anywhere from $149.95 plus tax to . . .

Mama had surely done her homework, thought Minna.

　. . . $900.00 for the more expensive. And there are word processors. As for moths, I have consulted several science books, but need more information . . .

The letter stopped there, and it came to Minna in that moment, quite suddenly, that her mother had not gone shopping at all. She had gone to the library to look up moths. To find the answers.

Minna skimmed her hands quickly, gently, over the typewriter keys. There were several other letters on the table.

Dear Mrs. Pratt,
    I love all your books but one.
                Please write back,
                Emma Jane Van Winkle

Dear Mrs. Pratt,
    My dog, Frank, ate page 27 of your book *A Day in the Life of Petunia*. Did I miss much?
                Respectfully yours,
                Tuli Kiplinger

Dear Mrs. Pratt,
    Do you ever get ideas from your children? My mother says she gets lots of ideas from me. If you need some ideas I'm sure she will send them to you.
                Best regards to your family and to
                your pet (if you have one),
                Maurice Choi
P.S. My lizard, Lurlene, died yesterday.

Answers, answers. Questions and answers. Do you get ideas from your family? Writers have all the answers. Minna stared at the typewriter. It was quiet in the mess. Peace among the socks. Very carefully, Minna removed her mother's letter about typewriters and moths and put in a fresh sheet of paper. She thought a moment, her fingers frozen above the keys. Dear Mama. No. She took a breath. And then, with two fingers, very slowly, she began to type.

Dear Mrs. Pratt,

A door slammed. The front door. It was the exuberant sound of her mother returning. Her mother had never been known to close a door quietly. How much time had gone by? Quickly Minna rolled the letter to her mother out of the typewriter, folded it, and put it safely in her pocket.

Downstairs in the kitchen, Emily Parmalee washed dishes, the suds up to her elbows. Minna's mother was unloading books from her book bag. McGrew was reading his science report to them.

"The beaver," he read, "uses his teeth for several reasons. One, to eat trees. Two, because of nervous energy. Last and least, to shine his teeth. Shiny teeth are highly valued in the beaver community."

Emily Parmalee and Minna's mother burst into laughter.

"Where did you get those facts?" asked Emily, scratching her nose and leaving a spot of suds there. "Did you interview a beaver?"

"I made them up," said McGrew, looking pleased. "What do you think?"

"McGrew, you can't make up facts!" Minna protested. She thought of Imelda's facts. The researched facts. *The truths*. "Made-up facts are not true," she said, exasperated.

Minna's mother leaned the broom against the wall and folded her arms.

"But Mama makes up facts," said McGrew. "In her books. I can, too."

"That's fiction!" said Minna, her voice rising. "It's not true!"

"It's about people and feelings and places," said McGrew, "and all those things are true."

Minna thought suddenly about the sign over her mother's desk. FACT AND FICTION ARE DIFFERENT TRUTHS. She thought about the letter folded in her pocket, full of feelings and facts about the person who was truly Minna Pratt though the letter could not be signed by her. "Truths, untruths; facts, fictions."

Her mother put her hand on Minna's shoulder, and Minna realized she had spoken the last out loud.

"Don't you remember, Minna, when you were five?" said her mother. "I once said to you, 'Is that

---

65

true, Minna?' and you answered, 'It's *one* of the truths, Mama!' "

There was silence then. Minna stared at her mother. What did I know then, thought Minna, that I've forgotten?

"One kind of truth, Min," her mother said. "A different kind."

She looked at McGrew. "And not," she said sternly, "for a science report."

"Unless you interview a beaver," repeated Emily Parmalee, scouring out the bean pot, making them smile.

Minna leaves them with their truths and soapsuds and beavers. She goes up the stairs, past her father's study, where he is singing. He does not sing well most times, except every so often when he happens on a beautiful note or two. As she listens he sings a phrase from *La Traviata*, his favorite opera. It is a long and lovely phrase, a sad phrase, that he sings to his books and papers. He does not see her, but she smiles at him, then leaves quickly before he sings badly again. His voice follows her down the hall.

> . . . *Misterioso, misterioso, altero,*
> *croce, croce e delizia*
> *croce e delizia, delizia al cor.*

In her room Minna takes out the letter to her mother.

> Dear Mrs. Pratt,
>   My mother doesn't really hear what I say.
> She doesn't listen. She asks me the wrong
> questions. She answers with wrong
> answers.

The letter is not yet signed. Minna slips the letter under her pillow, and that night she dreams about truths and untruths, facts and fictions. They are, all of them, dressed in furry suits and they scurry about the woods chewing on trees. *"Misterioso,"* they sing as they run from tree to tree. *"Misterioso."* If she looks closely Minna can see they are beavers. They have shiny teeth, highly valued in the beaver community.

NINE

*I*t is a cloudless day and the bus is full of excitement. Lewis's baby has been born.

"Beautiful she is!" Lewis exclaims to everyone who boards the bus. "Have a cigar. Fifty-five cents, please, exact change, please. Beautiful she is!"

McGrew gives his cigar to Emily Parmalee, who takes the paper cigar ring off and puts it on her finger. Minna zips her cigar into the music pocket of her cello case. Next to her letter. The letter has traveled everywhere with Minna: in her pocket, once barely saved from the laundry; in her case nestled next to Mozart. It is a troublesome reminder, like a spot of soot in her eye or a stone in her sock. Yet it is also a comfort, like the gargoyles. Like Willie, who is always there. Sometimes the sight of it makes Minna smile, the rustle of it settles her mind, its truths please her. The letter is neatly addressed to her mother, but there is still no signature. Signing the letter is a problem, though it hasn't always been a problem. For years Minna has been writing to people, some of them well known, using her own address and names she has borrowed or invented: Phoebe Crosstitch, Portia Puce, Veronica Jell.

Dear Leonard Bernstein,
    Your hair moves nicely when you conduct. . . .

Dear Mr. Baryshnikov,
    Your legs are very excellent. . . .

"Why?" asked her mother, mystified. "Why don't you sign your own name? Don't you want people to know who you are?"

"No," said Minna, knowing her mother didn't understand. Her mother wrote all kinds of personal things in her books, some of them embarrassing, and her mother didn't care. But Minna cared.

Dear Portia,
    Thank you for your letter regarding my hair. Do you prefer it when I conduct Stravinsky or when I do Debussy?

Dear Ms. Jell,
    As Mr. Baryshnikov's secretary I am writing to thank you on his behalf for your favorable comments on his legs. . . .

Easy names for those letters. But not for this one. Her own address for those letters. Not for this letter.

"Beautiful she is." Lewis's voice intruded on Minna's thoughts. "Nine pounds and a bit more."

Minna leaned forward.

"What's her name?" she asked suddenly.

"Eliza," said Lewis, smiling. "Sturdy little thing, with a face like the night moon."

Minna smiled at his poetry. And a good stout name, too, at last, she thought. After a moment she unzipped the pocket of her cello case and took out her letter. She glanced at McGrew to make sure he wasn't paying attention to her. He wasn't. He was stretched across the aisle singing headlines to Emily Parmalee and a surprisingly undersized woman in a white turban and a fur coat.

"Man Weds Horse," he sang. "Pinching Your Nose Increases Your I.Q."

Very carefully, Minna signed the typewritten letter. She wrote a script that was tall and straight, unlike her own writing:

Yours very truly,

Eliza Moon

A nice name, her mother would say.

"Is that true?" A voice spoke close to her ear.

Startled, Minna slid the letter into her coat pocket and turned around.

"What? Is what true?" she asked.

Behind her an old man leaned over the back of her seat.

"That," he whispered, "what the boy there said. Is it a fact? Pinching your nose makes you intelligent?"

Minna looked at McGrew. McGrew and Emily Parmalee sat, holding their noses, reading. Behind them sat a busful of passengers, all holding *their* noses.

"I'd believe it for a fact," Minna told the man. "That boy knows nearly everything." She faced front again. And what he doesn't know he makes up, she added to herself, thinking about his science report. The bus lurched to a stop, the door opening.

"Fifty-five cents, please. Exact change, please. She's born!" Lewis chanted to a new passenger. "Beautiful she is!"

The bus ground up again and Minna smiled at the look of the man as he walked up the aisle, his hand immediately flying up to pinch his nose, too.

"Does something smell?" he asked in a high nasal voice.

Willie was not on his street corner, but the dog was, as if waiting patiently for his instrument to be delivered to him. He greeted her with a crooked dog smile. When Minna reached down to pat him he lifted his head to meet her hand and smacked his tail against the pavement.

"Where's Willie?" Minna whispered to him. "Where?" She looked down the street. Maybe he had chosen another place to play. No, he wouldn't have done that. This was his place; here by the conservatory steps, by the gargoyles. Near the dog.

"Two-hour rehearsal today," Minna called to McGrew and Emily Parmalee.

"Yep," said McGrew. "We're going to the movies."

They sat for a moment, their backs against the building, and the dog collapsed in a fury of friendliness against them. Minna looked around once more for Willie, then she dragged her cello up the steps.

Hello, gargoyles. Hello, door. Hello, stairs. *Hello, Mozart.*

Upstairs it is not peaceful. Lucas has a buzz in his viola and he loosens and tightens strings. Orson has lost his music. He crouches over his case like a dog unearthing a buried bone, music flying out behind him. Haydn, Schumann, Donizetti, a piece of Ives flies by. No Mozart. Imelda sits peacefully, the eye of a storm. A muscle in Porch's cheek twitches and his eyes are dark.

"Aha!" exclaims Orson, straightening up with Mozart clutched in his hand.

The buzz stops when Lucas adjusts his bridge. Minna unzips her case and pulls out her cello.

"Do not threap us, we are ready," pronounces Orson. "Scold, that means," he tells Porch.

Porch smiles suddenly and they all smile back.

"Four weeks," says Porch. "An A please. C scale, then G."

Love, thinks Minna, peering at Lucas, who smiles a bright smile at her. *Surely love is a fact.* She misses a note and Porch points to her and glares. She glares back and stretches her fingers, furiously attacking the repeat of the andante. Porch nods and beckons her to play louder, stronger. She does and he grins. *Love.*

Cheerfully Porch loads them all into the elevator. Inside Minna leans back and closes her eyes as the elevator starts downward. Next to her Lucas stands close and his fingers drum the beginning measures of the presto on her hand. She smiles, her eyes still closed.

"I wonder," says Imelda, "if we have to wear uniforms for the concert. You know, dress alike."

"It's not baseball, Imelda," says Orson.

"I wish it were," says Minna, opening her eyes.

"It's a little like baseball," says Lucas, thoughtfully. "Everything has its own rhythms, I guess."

Minna closes her eyes again.

———

ANNOUNCER: *Welcome, baseball fans, on a beautiful sunny afternoon where the Sox are here to play Mozart. Playing first fiddle is number 7 . . . the shortstop will play second . . . the left fielder will hum.*

Downstairs, Willie had joined the dog.

"Willie!" called Minna.

Willie looked up from his tuning and smiled at her, surprised at her voice.

It was clear the dog loved Willie. He sat on Willie's shoe as Willie began a mazurka, wagging his tail just out of time, a little on the slow side, like a stubborn metronome. He slipped in and out of the crowd when Willie had finished and watched the listeners toss coins in Willie's case.

Minna fished a quarter out of her pocket and handed it to Willie.

"Thanks."

Willie bowed and handed it back.

"Thank *you*."

The dog whined, and Minna reached out and scratched his ears. He had wisps of brown hair that stuck out above his eyes and around his chin.

"He looks like an unfinished painting," said Lucas. "You know, not all smoothed and complete?"

Like me, thought Minna suddenly.

"You know, you're right," said Willie, looking down at the dog. "I wonder if he's mine."

Minna and Lucas laughed.

"What I mean," said Willie, "is that he's been here for days. He has no collar, no tags. I've been feeding him. He loves Mozart," added Willie. "My favorite, too."

Willie stuck his fiddle under his chin and played Schubert. The dog lay down. Willie played Tchaikovsky. The dog yawned and stretched. Willie played Mozart and the dog sat up, wagging his tail.

"That's it, then," said Willie, grinning. "His name is Mozart and he's mine. Just to keep it simple," he said to Minna, "I'll call him Dog."

So simple. Minna wished that everything were that simple; her mother, her father, her vibrato, her life. Maybe it was Willie who was that simple. That must be it. The rest of the world—*my* world—whirls and dips and turns inside out. But Willie is simple, dependable. Like a fact.

"Willie?" Minna could see McGrew and Emily way off in the distance, walking toward them.

"What?"

"When did you get a vibrato?"

"Vibrato? It was like magic. Almost like magic. One day I was playing and it happened. Up to then I'd done everything I could think of." He peered down at Minna. "Mostly practice."

"Did you get frustrated? Angry?"

"No," said Willie, smiling broadly. "I just played!" There was a pause.

"Porch says it's like a light coming on over your head," said Minna.

"True, in a way," said Willie thoughtfully. "Sometimes it's unexpected. Almost natural and hardly noticed, like your eyebrows growing. And sometimes it comes as a great surprise after a lot of hard work." He stopped. "Like becoming an adult."

McGrew and Emily Parmalee came then, with popcorn from the movies.

"She cried," announced McGrew.

"Can you play 'Baby, Baby, You're My Life' in B-flat?" asked Emily Parmalee tearfully.

Willie could. And he did.

Magic. Light over the head. Eyebrows growing?

Lucas walked Minna to the bus.

"Phone if you get your vibrato," he called to her.

Minna waved good-bye from the bus window. Maybe it had nothing to do with organization, thought Minna. Maybe getting a vibrato had something to do with intelligence. She held her nose all the way home. Just in case.

TEN

The day was warm, though it had rained, and the grass had lost its winter brown that Minna loved. That brown, Minna thought, was the way the prairie would look. Lucas was coming to dinner tonight and Minna wished she were in the middle of the prairie, or perhaps sitting on the continental divide, just she and Lucas with a campfire and Devil Dogs for dessert. They would make wise and witty conversation in complete sentences with big words, adverbial phrases, and commas. Maybe even semicolons. Not conversations like her parents had at dinner, full of dashes and hyphens.

"I saw Mrs. You Know Who today—whatshername?"

"Ah yes—in all her glory?"

"Mr. Thing was with her—"

"With his great drooling dog, I betcha."

"Shoot the potatoes down here—will you, luv?"

Luv. Her mother and father wrote notes to each other, almost always signing them "luv." They kissed often, not only in the kitchen and in the quiet hallways of the house, but in the yard. Once she had seen them on the street, leaning against a tree, their arms around each other, kissing directly on the mouth for a great long time as if her father might be going off to war. Minna had been with McGrew and Emily Parmalee, who had been fascinated, mostly by the breathing techniques involved in such a long kiss.

"Do they breathe through their noses, or do they leave a bit of free space at the edges of their mouths, do you think?" Emily Parmalee asked, amazed. "My parents never kiss long enough to run out of air."

"I imagine that they take a great gulping breath before they do it," said McGrew, not embarrassed like Minna. "Though it's hard to say. We could try."

And they had, right there on the sidewalk in daylight, smashed their lips together while people walked by smiling and a cat, its tail in the air, stopped to peer up at them. Mortified, Minna felt surrounded by kissers. Afterward, McGrew and Emily had agreed that taking a breath didn't work.

"You have to blow it out suddenly," explained Emily, "you know, explode on your partner's mouth."

Minna shrugged away the memory and dragged her cello down the hallway, pausing outside her mother's writing room.

"Lucas for dinner tonight," she reminded her mother.

"I hope he's plump and tender," joked her mother, not looking up.

"Mother."

"Okay, sweetie. We'll have stew instead."

"And no tofu," said Minna. "Or hamburger pickles."

"Check, luv," said her mother, leaning over her typewriter to pen in a correction.

"Mother," said Minna softly. "I want this to be a special dinner."

"Um," said her mother, her voice coming from somewhere far away. She stared at her page.

"Mother," repeated Minna. "You're not paying attention to me. Mother?"

Silence.

It is then, at that very moment, her mother's head bent over the typewriter, Minna's arm draped around her cello, that Minna's anger overtakes her. It is like a spilled drink, the anger that flows over her. She leans her cello against the wall in the hallway, walks down the stairs, her face grim, and walks out the door to the mailbox. She passes the Parmalee house, crisp and still in its neatness; passes the big tree where her parents have lately kissed, and drops her letter without a return address into the mailbox. With a clatter of the mailbox door it is gone. Minna stands there for a moment, both frightened and pleased. Then she walks back past the tree, past the Parmalee house, back to the upstairs hallway, where her cello waits in its case. Her mother is still hunched over the typewriter, her back to Minna.

Frowning, Minna walked down the hall, down the stairs, through the dining room to her father's office. The door was open and her father was inside, his feet up on his desk, conducting the Triumphal March from *Aida*. Minna slipped in and sat, waiting for the end. She looked around. It was a peaceful room, with comfortable chairs and book-lined walls. Full of facts, thought Minna. There are many facts here, many truths. Does my father know all these facts?

The music ended and her father looked up.

"I did that well, don't you think?" he asked her, smiling.

Minna nodded.

"Could we, do you think," she began slowly. She paused.

"Clean up the house?" her father finished for her.

"Could we?" asked Minna eagerly. "Could *you*?" she added because she was off, it suddenly occurred to her, to play Mozart, whom she could never play as right, as perfectly, as her father's recordings. "We're having Lucas for dinner tonight, Papa."

Her father got up and came over to her. He put his arm around her.

"I hope," he said.

Minna knew what he was about to say.

"That he is . . ." her father went on.

"Plump and tender," whispered Minna before her father could finish.

Her father smiles at her. Minna does not smile back. She is weary of his smiles. She suddenly wishes that she had a letter in her pocket to mail to her father, return address and name unknown. Then, at the door, she decides on something better. She turns.

"You should, you know," she says in a high clear voice, "teach your son McGrew how to catch a fly ball."

Surprised, her father looks up. Before he can speak she is gone.

Minna carries her cello outside, where Emily Parmalee is hitting fungoes to McGrew in the side yard. She watches McGrew miss every ball that comes to him. Unexpected tears sting her eyes.

Emily has startling rhinestone earrings on today, shaped like chandeliers.

"They belonged to my great aunt Lila," she calls to Minna, who admires them from the steps. "She died in the bathtub with them on."

Minna believes that. They are huge and long, swaying heavily as Emily swings the baseball bat. They probably pulled Aunt Lila to the bottom of the tub, under the water.

The bus pulls up to the curb, the doors opening for her. Minna leans her cello on the seat next to her and practices her vibrato on her knee. She can do it on her knee and on the dining room table and on her nightstand. After what she has just done— mailing a letter to her mother, telling her father what she has always wished to tell him—perhaps she will suddenly and magically be able to do it on her cello. Minna sighs. Right now the only place she can't do her vibrato is on her cello. She feels like a surgeon who can only carve turkeys, or a prima ballerina who only dances in her dreams.

Willie and Dog were playing Schubert. Rather, Willie was playing and Dog was looking smug and patient as he waited for Mozart. When Willie finished he nodded, and the listeners applauded and tossed coins. One man had brought Dog a biscuit.

"Nice," said Minna. She handed Willie thirteen cents from her pocket.

He dropped it back into her hand.

"We thank you, Dog and I," he said solemnly. "Any luck yet?" he asked. She knew what he meant.

"Nope. No light over my head."

"Don't work so hard," said Willie, wiping rosin from his violin. "Think about the music, not just the notes. It will creep up on you, like moonlight."

The music, not the notes. Weren't they the same? Minna frowned. Everyone she knew spoke words she did not understand. Moonlight? No moonlight here, thought Minna.

"Good-bye, Willie." She leaned down to touch Dog. "Good-bye, Dog," she whispered.

Willie tuned and began to play again. Minna pushed the great door open and trudged up the stairs after a quick glance at the elevator. Old habits, the stairs. Wasn't there a saying about that? About old dogs and old habits? Or was it old dogs and new tricks? Minna felt like an old dog. Sadly she climbed the stairs, for the first time forgetting to look up at the gray gargoyles. She remembered halfway up the stairs, hesitated, then, leaving her cello stranded on the landing, dashed down and out to look at them for luck.

Upstairs Porch was cross, out of sorts in a great oppressive, sighing kind of way.

"Porch's in a bilious mood," whispered Orson, barely moving his lips as he spoke. "Irritable."

"You're on time," said Imelda in a soft voice. "It is said that punctuality reflects an orderly mind."

Hush, said Minna in her head as she smiled at Lucas.

"Now," said Porch, "in all honesty have you practiced?"

"In all honesty I have practiced," said Lucas, smiling broadly.

"In all honesty I have practiced," said Imelda smugly.

"In all honesty I have practiced," said Minna, grinning at Porch.

"In all honesty I have practiced and it has made little difference," said Orson, making them laugh.

"Three weeks," announced Porch, sitting down. "Let's have an A, then a G-major scale. *Then* we'll begin with K. 156. You know it well." He peered over his glasses. "Therefore you can play it bee-uu-tee-fullee."

There are times, more often lately, that Minna feels she knows Mozart better than she knows herself. Mozart is everywhere, like the wind. She catches one of his phrases in her teacher's voice, in the rhythms of the jump rope rhymes when the neighborhood children play. One morning, early, the garbage men outside bang their way into the *Hunt Quartet,* causing Minna to sit straight up in bed, wide awake.

She slips into the presto of K. 156 as easily as sliding into her shoes without looking. The adagio in its slow sweet walk into the minuetto is as close and familiar to her as her skin.

"Now that is good!" says Porch dramatically when they are finished.

"Then why can't we play this for the competition?" asks Imelda.

"Because you know it so well that you don't work at it," says Porch promptly. "You play it with a yawn. That was catsup. Now let's see blood. K. 157, everyone. Second position in the andante, Minna. Blood, remember!"

Minna places her bow on the strings.

Dear Mrs. Pratt, she composes in her head. *Help. My life is full of parents and sharps and flats and high third fingers. And other messes, too,* she adds. *Like blood.*

ELEVEN

The elevator, to everyone's surprise, was not working. A small sign taped to the door read "Out of Odor." Orson unearthed a pen and squeezed in an *r*, satisfied. "Out of Ordor." Imelda surprised them all. "There is often," she said, "no room for perfection in an imperfect world."

They trooped down the flights of stone stairs out into the light, where Willie was playing a piece that Minna didn't recognize. She poked Lucas.

"Bach," he said.

They sat on the steps to wait for Twig to pick them up and drive them to Minna's house for dinner. Minna leaned back against the building and watched Willie. He had a smile on his face and he played without looking at the strings. Minna knew he was not even aware of the crowd listening, or of Dog leaning up against his legs. It was peaceful and the music seemed to close them all in, capturing them. Minna thought of Mr. and Mrs. Ellerby and their conversation at dinner, soft and serene, like Debussy. Willie's fingers vibrated on the violin strings. Dog closed his eyes.

Suddenly Twig arrives with a screech of brakes. She is driving a long black car and she runs up on the curb, knocking over a wire trash basket. The crowd turns around. Willie stops playing. Willie never stops playing in noise and confusion. Minna remembers a car catching on fire once, Willie playing through the sirens of the fire truck.

Twig appears from the depths of the car.

"Are you all right?" calls Willie.

"Certainly," says Twig. She frowns. "Though I think I have torn a fender."

"This is Twig," says Lucas, introducing them. "Twig lives at my house."

"I am the Ellerbys' housekeeper," says Twig.

"And . . . ?" says Willie.

Twig cocks her head to one side.

"Surely there's more," says Willie. He grins at her suddenly. "I'm William Gray." He extends his hand. "Willie."

Twig smiles.

"Yes," she says, taking his hand. "There is more. I'm housekeeping to earn money to finish school.

My family lives in Vermont, and I'm thinking about art school."

Lucas looks at Minna.

"I never knew that," he says softly.

Minna nods.

After a moment Willie drops Twig's hand to pull Dog from the trash basket, where he has found half a cupcake. Twig turns to Lucas.

"Why don't you put the instruments in the car. Yourselves in the front. I'll be there in a moment."

She turns back to Willie.

"My family has a farm; they raise sheep for wool, you know."

"I didn't know she came from Vermont," grumbles Lucas as they put the cello on the floor of the car, the viola on the seat.

"I didn't know about the sheep, either," he mutters as they climb into the front seat and watch through the window. "Or art school!"

"My mother would have known," Minna says suddenly. She turns to look at Lucas. "She asks questions. My mother does."

Lucas sighs.

"Mine doesn't," he says so sadly that Minna reaches over to take his hand.

Outside Twig leans against the hood of the car. Willie smiles and brushes hair off his forehead. Dog watches them.

"I wonder where Willie lives now," says Minna.

"He talked about his mother once. I wonder where she lives."

Beside her Lucas shakes his head. They stare out the window for a long time. Finally, Willie goes back to his Bach, lifting his violin good-bye to them. Twig climbs in the car.

"Nice man," says Twig. "Lives on Fourteenth Street. Has six sisters. His mama lives on a farm in Iowa."

Lucas nudges Minna and she grins as Willie begins to play, and suddenly the peace is over. Twig is a terrible driver, speeding up behind cars and stopping so that Lucas and Minna are rocked back and forth. Twig slams the car into gear, reminding Minna of her mother slapping the eraser cartridge into her typewriter.

"Road toad!" yells Twig. "Move it or park it!"

She weaves in and out of traffic and Minna glances quickly at Lucas. His eyes are closed. Minna closes her eyes and clenches her hands in her lap, but it doesn't help. She pictures Twig housecleaning with the same fury, shoving aside tables and chairs, the vacuum cleaner like a sword cutting swatches through the furniture and mounds of dirt. Death to dust balls! Down with detritus! A new word, detritus, that Orson has taught them. It refers to all the clutter in his violin case: the papers and cookie crumbs, rubber bands, half-eaten apples, and the old T-shirt that he uses to cover his instrument.

It would take Twig about forty-seven minutes, thinks Minna, to put her mother's house in order, sucking up dust balls and crumpled pages that surround her mother's desk like mushrooms growing randomly on a lawn. A vision of gleaming pots and pans and furniture smelling of lemons makes Minna open her eyes again. They've nearly reached her street.

"Turn left here," says Minna quickly, and Twig wheels left through a yellow light. The viola case falls off the backseat and hits the floor with a thump.

"On the right there," says Minna. "The front porch with the green trash bags. . . . "

Twig nods and whips around a car that is double parked and screeches to a stop in front of Minna's house. On the sidewalk stand McGrew and Emily Parmalee, their mouths slightly open as they stare at the car. Twig shuts off the motor and the engine rattles on a bit, then stops. Silence fills the car. Minna begins to count her breaths.

"Should I bring in my viola?" asked Lucas on the street. "We could practice some after dinner."

Minna hesitated, then nodded.

"I suppose."

Emily Parmalee and McGrew were playing hopscotch on the front walk.

"See?" said Minna to Lucas. "Hopscotch."

"I'm Emily," announced Emily, shaking hands

with Twig. "That's McGrew about to step on a line."

"No, I'm not," sang McGrew. "Most often I win."

"Well," said Twig, "the opera's not over 'til the fat lady sings."

McGrew looked up from square three.

"Is that a headline?" he asked.

Twig shook her head.

"It's a saying," she said. "It means the game's not over yet. It means there is more."

A fact, thought Minna.

McGrew smiled and moved slightly, stepping on a line.

"Now, for the fat lady!" said Emily Parmalee, tossing down her stone.

"I'll pick you up later," said Twig, her hand on Lucas's shoulder.

They watched her roar off, straight out from the curb, leaving a honking of horns behind her.

"You never told me about her driving," said Minna after a moment.

Beside her, Lucas lifted his shoulders in a half shrug.

"That is because," he said, "there are no words for it."

"It is true, very true," sang Emily Parmalee behind them, sounding very much like McGrew, "that the fat lady is winning."

Laughing, Minna and Lucas walked inside.

Lucas loves Minna's parents on sight. Minna can tell. He follows her mother and father around like Dog follows Willie. Verdi composed *his* favorite operas, he tells Minna's father. Her father beams. He looks over her mother's shoulder in the kitchen, reading the cookbook. Her mother is actually cooking something out of a book, a meat and potato dish with a "garnish" of parsley, as the book says.

"I don't have fresh parsley," her mother complains. "Things I cook never look like these pictures."

"No," agrees Lucas kindly, and Minna suddenly thinks of how beautiful Twig's dishes are, like small paintings ready to be framed in gilt. "I heard," Lucas continues, "that they prop up the vegetables and meats in stews with toothpicks or old rags before they're photographed."

Minna's parents laugh. Minna can see that her mother likes Lucas for that alone.

The dining room has been packed into boxes along one wall. At least the clutter that is usually the dining room table is in boxes and there are candles and two extra places, one for Lucas, another for Emily Parmalee. If Minna squints her eyes just right it looks like a nicely set table in a room where someone is either moving in or moving out.

Dinner conversation is as always, though no one

"shoots" the potatoes. Lucas spends a good deal of the meal with his fork suspended in the air, turning his head from one end of the table to the other as if he is watching a long rally in tennis. He has a dazed, dim-witted look on his face. When dessert is finally served, it is amidst a heated argument between Emily Parmalee and McGrew about their favorite headline of the day. Emily likes TALK SHOW HOST FINDS LIFE'S MEANING IN A FORTUNE COOKIE. McGrew prefers RACCOONS DELIVER $100,000 IN COINS TO POOR MINNESOTA WIDOW. Lucas loves the raccoon headline.

Dessert is something Minna doesn't recognize, a hodgepodge of something.

"Trifle!" exclaims Lucas happily as Minna's father sets it on the table. He smiles at it as if greeting an ancient friend from a past life.

"Right-o, you betcha, luv," says Minna's mother, smiling, switching on the overhead light to illuminate the room in all its horror.

At that moment, Minna abandons all hope of serene candlelight dinners, soft talk, and meaningful conversation with topics and subtopics. Forever.

It was quiet, dinner finished, Minna's father gone to his study. Lucas followed Minna's mother into her writing room to read the first three pages of her new book. Minna sat next to Lucas and listened to their discussion of names. In an absentminded gesture Lucas reached into the laundry basket and matched a pair of socks, then another.

"I would have liked the name Luther better than Lucas, actually," he said to her mother. "It's something about the *r* at the end."

"You may be right," said Minna's mother. She leaned over to write the name "Luther" on a notepad.

Lucas placed the sock balls on the table and looked at Minna's mother apologetically.

"There are no more mates here," he announced.

There was a silence.

"None at all?" asked her mother, surprised.

Minna stared at the two of them, fascinated. It was as if they were discussing the plotting of a book, or a character. Or where to set the story. In the forest? By the sea?

"As I see it," said Lucas matter-of-factly, "these can simply be thrown out. Unless, of course," he added, "there is another basket just like this one somewhere."

Minna's mother smiled a great smile and stood, as if she might be about to knight Lucas.

Thrown out. Who else but Lucas could have unearthed such a simple solution for the tumble of socks? Had they all been waiting for them—the socks—to be reunited after years apart? To mate, perhaps, and have small matching offspring? Minna sighed. Something was wrong. Lucas should live here. And I should live in the grand house where dinner conversation can be divided into headings on three-by-five cards, all lined.

1. Oil
    A. Origins and location of
    B. Transportation of
    C. Price of

Minna's mother dumped the entire basket of socks in her tall wastebasket.

"There! Thank you, luv," she said to Lucas.

Down the hallway there was music from her father's study. Lucas peered in at Minna's father from the doorway.

"Don Giovanni?"

Minna's father, in a frenzy of conducting, nodded and smiled without missing a beat.

"Shall we practice?" Lucas asked Minna as they walked on down the hallway.

Minna sighed.

"The andante, maybe?" she said wistfully. "Slow and peaceful?"

"Right-o, you betcha," murmured Lucas, opening his viola case. "Luv."

They sit across from each other, singing the parts they don't play. It is quiet and strangely eerie, the two parts playing, the ghosts of Imelda and Orson and Porch lurking nearby. WA Mozart "hoovering," as Twig would say it, above them all.

If this were a story, thinks Minna; if this were fiction, this is where I'd finally get my vibrato, sitting across from Lucas, who has just called me "luv." But it is her mother who is the writer of fiction, not Minna. And it does not happen.

"Nice," says Lucas when they finish. "And in tune." He leans back in his chair.

There is, at that moment, a squeal of brakes outside, a sound of scraping metal. Lucas and Minna sit silently.

McGrew pushes the door open.

"I think Twig might be here," he whispers. "What's funny?" he asks as they burst into laughter. Minna drops her bow and leans, breathless, over her cello.

"Mozart?" asks McGrew, mystified. He moves quickly into the room to peer at their music. "Mozart's *funny*?!"

TWELVE

On Wednesday three bad things happen. At school Miss Barbizon praises Minna's vocabulary story and puts it up on the bulletin board. Minna hates seeing her homework on the bulletin board, her name and thoughts there for everyone to know. Miss Barbizon assigns new words for next week: *cachinnate, nettlesome, bogus, sibling, ozone*. Furious, Minna silently vows to use them all in one sentence for vengeance.

"And remember," cries Miss Barbizon, "a beginning, a middle, and . . ." The dismissal bell drowns out Miss Barbizon.

After school Minna's mother meets her at the front door with a letter in her hand. Minna's heart races. She has almost forgotten mailing the letter to her mother with the signature of Eliza Moon. But it is not that letter. It is something worse: an invitation from Porch to the competition at the concert hall.

"Why?" asks her mother angrily. "Why didn't you tell us?"

Minna is silent. Her mind whirls with explanations. I forgot. Didn't I tell you? I did, but you were too busy writing. You didn't hear. I wasn't sure of the date. I don't want you there. At last Minna decides on the truth.

"I don't really understand it," she says simply. "I'm not sure."

She waits, and then, to her amazement, her mother smiles.

"Well, then," she says.

Her mother turns and walks inside. Minna follows her. *Well then?*

"I can understand that, Min," says her mother. She sighs a small sigh and looks at Minna. "Do you mind if we're there, Dad and I? We'd like to hear you. We won't come if you don't want us to."

Minna takes a breath.

"I think I would like you to be there," says Minna, realizing to her great surprise that it is the second truth she has spoken in a few moments to her mother.

In the afternoon the worst thing happens. Minna has thought about this happening. She has thought about it every day, and when it happens it is just as bad as she could have imagined. Imelda comes to chamber group with a vibrato. Minna's heart sinks as she listens to Imelda's elaborate explanation. Imelda speaks in scattered italics.

"My aunt Fiona had just finished telling me how a *gypsy*, actually a *fortune teller*, had once read her palm and told her exactly when she'd meet the love of her life. When she *left* the fortune teller's shop she just *knew* she'd meet him . . ."

Orson yawns. Lucas shifts a bit in his chair. Porch smiles at Minna.

". . . and she *did*. At *that* moment, that *very* moment that she's telling me the *story* I just *know* that my vibrato will come to me if I *practice*. I *practice*. And it *does*!" Imelda beams.

"Very *nice*," says Porch, unconsciously continuing the italics. "One *must*, however," he cautions her, "be *careful* not to let a *vibrato* mask playing in *tune*."

Good Old Back Porch, thinks Minna.

"A sapient word," says Orson. "Wise," he pronounces to the Mozart on his stand.

"And speaking of playing in tune," says Porch, "let's begin today with scales. C, then F, then G."

"Scales!" cries Imelda. "But I've got a vibrato!"

"Give me an A now," says Porch rather sharply. "Scales first, then some Haydn before we cause Mozart great anguish."

"He died, you know, at thirty-five," states Imelda darkly.

"And I," says Porch with a sigh, "know exactly how he felt before it happened."

Minna loves scales. When played in tune they are simple and predictable, like facts. Even the slightest bit out of tune they are horrid and uncertain. Playing them, thinks Minna, is a little like walking a tightrope: there are no safe spaces on each side if you wobble over. And Imelda is wobbling. Porch gives her a cross look, pointing a finger at her. Orson, not paying attention, begins to play faster than the rest. Porch steps on his foot and Orson looks up surprised. Haydn is better, though not in tune at times. At last Porch explodes.

"I feel like I'm walking four dogs at the same time," he says loudly. "One short-legged, one long-legged, one old and decrepit, and one just plain foolish!" He points at Orson. "You are not listening. Imelda, you are in love with your vibrato. Minna and Lucas, your minds are elsewhere. Up, up!" Porch waves his arms. They stand, and he moves their music stands and chairs so that they face different parts of the room. "Now sit. And play the music. The music! Not just what you see or don't see in front of you!" They sit with their backs to each other. Lucas faces the window, Imelda the wall, Orson the closet. Minna plays to the hall-way door.

"Now," says Porch, "Mozart." He holds up his hand. "Two weeks," he says softly.

Poor Porch, thinks Minna, studying the panels of the door. He should be coaching a recording like my father does. In tune always. Perfect always. But Porch isn't coaching a recording. It is, Minna remembers Imelda's words, an imperfect world after all.

Dear Mrs. Pratt, begins Minna in her head. She stops.

"Ready," says Porch in a low voice.

Minna places her bow on the strings.

Dear Mrs. Pratt? No, not Mrs. Pratt. It occurs to Minna, just before Porch says "play," that she has no cross words left for Mrs. Pratt. She has already mailed her angry letter. It is done with, her anger, disappearing into the mailbox. It is gone like an old wart or hair too long, or an ugly pair of shoes Minna once quietly slipped far under the seat of the bus on her way home from a lesson.

"Lost?" her mother had cried, incredulous. "How can you lose your shoes?"

"Play," says Porch.

They begin. In tune. Minna smiles at her music. She has found someone else for complaints, some-one close, someone more than close. Someone everywhere these days, like the wind.

Dear WA Mozart, Minna begins, *You probably don't know me . . .*

"Aha!" exclaimed Porch when they had finished the presto. "I am a genius chamber music coach! It's working, can you hear it? Yes, you *do* hear it. Mozart hears it, too, and I know for a fact that he loves it. We'll practice this way all the time!"

There was much grumbling as they packed up their instruments and walked to the elevator.

"It's boring facing the closet," said Orson. "And eerie. I keep picturing Mozart sitting in there, crouched among leftover boots and bumbershoots—that's umbrellas—holding his ears."

Imelda said nothing.

"Porch is right," said Lucas thoughtfully. "We sounded better."

Minna nodded as he pushed the elevator button and found the elevator was back in order. It was true. Perhaps it was more musical to play to the door, not catching sight of Orson rolling his eyes at her, not smiling at Lucas, not eyeing Imelda's vibrato with envy.

"I like it," said Minna. "It's private." *Just Mozart and Minna Pratt.*

"It's unnatural," announced Imelda, breaking her silence. "Can you imagine the Juilliard Quartet facing the wall? Or the Guarneri playing Schubert to a closet? Or," her voice rose and her face reddened, "Itzhak Perlman performing for a radiator?!"

"With or without a vibrato?" asked Orson with a smile.

The elevator doors opened and Imelda marched out, ignoring them.

"What a galoot," said Orson, shaking his head. "That means . . ."

"Silly," said Lucas and Minna at the same time, looking at each other with surprise, linking little fingers.

Outside Willie was playing a Beethoven minuet. Twig waved to them. Dog was busy nosing the picnic basket at her feet.

"Dear Wolfgang," says Minna out loud on the bus, startling the woman next to her. *Dear Wolfgang,* she repeats silently.

No offense, Wolfgang, but since you were
a violinist as well as a pianist I am sure you had
to worry about your vibrato. Please help me
find mine. It does concern your music, after all.
K. 157, if it makes a difference. You know
that hard part. You wrote it. Please help me.
                    Minna Pratt
P.S. I already tried God.

THIRTEEN

*O*ne week. *Do you hear that, Wolfgang?* A full week of practice every day they've had, with the next week to be the same. All this time Minna has become well acquainted with the door to the rehearsal room: the moldings, the panels, the hinges, the dull brass doorknob. She knows each scratch and blemish as well as she knows her own. She has also become well acquainted with the music, drawing it around her like a cloak that is large enough to contain the person inside. Minna Booth Pratt hidden in the package of Mozart. No vibrato.

Porch smiles almost every day. He has been nearly overcome with happiness. Minna tells her mother this and her mother smiles and writes down "nearly overcome."

"A wonderful phrase, Minna. Sounds like love."

Minna knows this and she says so.

"I know that."

"I am sure you do," says her mother, for once not turning back to her typewriter. She stares at Minna for so long that it is Minna who finally turns away.

In the middle of the week Porch invites a large serious woman with a long upper lip to sit in to listen. She is in charge of the competition. Her name is Mrs. Willoughby-Fiske with an *e*, Porch tells them. No one smiles. They play for her, and when they are finished she nods at them and applauds as they turn from their corners to look at her.

"Smart, aren't I?" says Porch excitedly. "Very, very, very smart. Very!" he adds as final punctuation. Minna makes a note to remember to use that many very's when Miss Barbizon asks for a one hundred word essay, "no more, no less!"

On Thursday, Minna writes her vocabulary words into one sentence. She has been working at it all week, thinking of it nearly as often as she thinks of Mozart and her vibrato. And Lucas. She shows it to him.

Although often <u>nettlesome</u> in many ways, my <u>bogus sibling</u> always manages to <u>cachinnate</u> at the fresh smell of <u>ozone</u> after a midsummer storm.

"I like it," says Lucas. "It is very clever and smart. It almost succeeds at meaning nothing."

"*Very* clever and smart?" asks Minna.

"Very, very, very clever and smart," says Lucas, smiling.

On Friday, Minna leaves the house to catch the bus. She stops, staring. Outside are Emily Parmalee, McGrew, and her father playing baseball. Her father has never spoken to her about helping McGrew. She had thought he didn't hear her. Emily Parmalee hits a high pop-up. McGrew is covering first base. Minna's father never reaches the ball. He stares upward at it for a long time, and when he decides to move he falls down. The ball drops beside him. McGrew and Emily Parmalee are kind.

"Nice try," says Emily.

"Keep your eye on the ball," calls McGrew, who has never, in Minna's memory, ever watched the baseballs that were hit to *him*.

"He is terrible at this," McGrew whispers to Minna.

"Very, very, very terrible," Minna whispers back.

One week, WA. I like your music, WA. Please, just the smallest hint, the tiniest wiggle of a vibrato, WA.

"Lovely, lovely," said Porch when they had finished. He grinned a grin that showed all his teeth. "Now, this week we will rehearse every day here, but once and only once at the hall next door."

The concert hall. *Is that where you are, Wolfgang?*

"And I want you to know how splendid you are. You have been playing the music! Mozart applauds you wherever he is."

"He's in the closet," said Orson.

"And," said Porch, ignoring Orson, "I want to remind you that winning the competition is not the important thing. Doing as well as you can is the important thing. Enjoying it. Not the money."

"Money was not important to Mozart," said Imelda, tapping one foot. "I read that Mozart and his wife danced once to keep warm when they had no heat and no money for fuel. Mozart himself was cheerful in his poverty."

"Go," said Porch, beginning to laugh. "Go." He waved them out.

Downstairs Minna and Lucas heard the sounds of Suzuki, and they paused at the door. A crowd of young violinists bowed away on *Perpetual Motion,* then *allegro.*

"Pizzicato!" called their teacher, her hair falling down from a bun. One child stopped bowing to scratch, another waved at Lucas, who waved back. The teacher frowned at them and closed the door. They stood quietly for a moment, Minna suddenly thinking of her small cello in the attic. The cello she would not play again.

Outside it was overcast, with a light that softened them all. Willie was not playing on the corner.

Instead, a girl was there, with long black hair, playing a flute. Her case was opened on the sidewalk, and in it was a hand-lettered sign that read FOR CAMP.

Willie was leaning up against the long black car talking to Twig. Minna saw that the torn fender of the car had been mended. A breeze rippled the flute player's hair. Dog lifted his leg over a white-walled tire to the clear notes of Ravel.

"You *are* coming to dinner tonight, aren't you?" asked Twig. "Do you want a ride?"

"No ride," said Minna quickly. "Thank you. We'll let you take the instruments. We'll walk."

The flutist packs up her flute and leaves. Willie takes out his violin and tunes, listening intently over his strings. Twig sits on the sidewalk under a small tree. Dog falls into her lap in a heap of love. Minna and Lucas walk slowly down the street, past the concert hall with its great arches. Soon Brahms overtakes them.

> *One week. Do you hear that, Wolfgang?*
> *A bargain, maybe? I have, as you may know,*
> *taught Lucas Ellerby how to play hopscotch.*
> *I am, as you may also know, playing in tune.*
> *A vibrato would be fine.*

At Lucas's house Mrs. Ellerby greets them at the door.

"Melinda! How nice."

Mrs. Ellerby wears a dress of many-colored explosions.

"We'll eat shortly."

Mr. Ellerby appears in gray.

"We are," he says formally, "very much looking forward to hearing you play. Our first invitation."

They disappear into the living room and Minna looks closely at Lucas.

"First invitation?" she asks. "You said they never came to hear you play. Ever."

Lucas sighed.

"What I didn't tell you was that I never invited them," he said softly. "You remember you once told me you didn't want your parents to come to hear you play because they'd make a fuss?"

Minna nodded.

"Well, I never invited them because . . . because I was afraid they *wouldn't* make a fuss," says Lucas, looking at the floor.

Minna puts her hand on his arm.

"They will," she whispers to Lucas. "I just know they'll make a fuss." After a moment Minna says it again. "They *will!*" she exclaims, making Lucas smile.

Minna dreams through another dinner at Lucas's, a dinner that has begun quietly but will soon erupt into a fuss that comes sooner than either of them has expected. Today the talk is of rugs: oriental versus wall-to-wall, with a small scuffle—so slight that Minna hardly notices—over something called a runner.

Flowered, do you think? asks Mrs. Ellerby.

Pale, perhaps, says Mr. Ellerby. So as not to overcome the portraits.

Minna looks across the table at Lucas, who rolls his eyes at her so that only the whites show. Minna smiles.

Twig, her cheeks pink, slips the salad plates on the table. As she leans over, Minna catches a scent of perfume. Lilac?

Minna eats the boneless chicken with sauce l'apricot and asparagus hollandaise as talk of fabric and rugs winds about her. Then, suddenly, in the midst of all the peace there is something wrong. The talk has changed.

"I'll just go up to the attic and fetch the fabric," says Mrs. Ellerby, standing. "I'm sure that's where Twig has put it."

"No," says Lucas. He stands, too.

Mr. Ellerby, his fork poised between plate and mouth, looks up, confused.

And it is then that Minna knows why Lucas's face is pale. The attic door is next to Lucas's room. *The frogs.*

"I'll go," says Lucas, moving toward the stairs.

"Sit, sit, sit," says Mrs. Ellerby, disappearing

out the door. "I'll be back in but a moment."

Twig swings through the doors and stops, staring at Minna and Lucas, standing.

"Ready for dessert?" she asks in an uncertain voice, looking from one to the other.

"Yes," says Lucas unsteadily, sitting.

Minna sits, too, but Mr. Ellerby has stood, so there is a moment of bobbing about the table. Minna feels a sudden surge of laughter rising, but she cannot laugh because of the stricken look on Lucas's face.

They will never have dessert. There will be no more comforting talk at the table, for after a moment Mrs. Ellerby stands in her explosive dress at the dining room door, her face dark.

"There are alien creatures up there," she says in a low voice. "Creatures!" Her voice fades to a whisper.

Mr. and Mrs. Ellerby will not allow arguments at the table so the "dialogue," as Mrs. Ellerby calls it, is moved to the hall. Minna follows them, disappointed. Her family often has arguments over dinner. They are full of energy and loud words. Once, Minna suddenly remembers, her mother threw a yam at her father and they both laughed.

"This cannot be allowed," says Mrs. Ellerby. "Go look, Frederick," she commands Mr. Ellerby.

"They are not alien creatures," protests Lucas.

"They are frogs, plain and simple. Mother, frogs were probably on this earth before humans, in one shape or another."

Mr. Ellerby appears at the top of the stairs looking grim.

"Those must go, Lucas," he says ominously.

"They are my pets," says Lucas as Mr. Ellerby descends the stairs. "I feed them. They are family!"

"They are *not* family," says Mrs. Ellerby firmly.

"They are family to me," says Lucas. "They feel like family. Look at Uncle Morton's portrait in the hallway. He even looks like a frog."

This is taken by Mr. and Mrs. Ellerby as an insult. Their faces close up tight.

"We are trying very hard," says Mr. Ellerby in a soft voice, "not to lose our tempers. The frogs must go."

There are no angry words, no raised voices, no tears. It is the worst argument Minna has ever heard.

Lucas bounds up the stairs, leaving Minna and Twig standing silently in the hallway.

"I am truly sorry for this disturbance," says Mrs. Ellerby to Minna. "You should have told us about the frogs," she tells Twig.

"We have a meeting, Melinda," says Mr. Ellerby. He shakes her hand. "So lovely to have had you for dinner."

The door opens. The door closes. *A disturbance?* Minna and Twig stare at each other.

"What now?" says Twig. "The pond, I suppose." She looks up the stairway. "Poor Lucas," she murmurs. "I tried to keep the frogs a secret. I knew how it would be."

Dear Mrs. Pratt, Minna begins automatically. She stops, her hand on her cheek.

"Minna?" asks Twig.

Minna smiles. *Dear Mrs. Pratt.*

"I know what to do," she says. "Not the pond. Not today, anyway. I know Lucas doesn't want to let them go yet. Could Willie help carry the tanks?"

"Of course," says Twig. "Where are the frogs going?"

Minna takes a deep breath and begins walking up the stairs.

"We'll see," says Minna without turning around.

Lucas is in his room staring at the frogs.

"Don't worry," says Minna in the doorway. "I have thought of something."

She picks up the phone.

"What something?" asks Lucas. "What?"

Minna shakes her head and dials.

"You'll see."

Minna waits.

"Hello," says her mother.

"Mother, I need your help. Without questions."

Minna hears the small clicking sound of her mother turning off her electric typewriter.

"Yes?"

"Lucas has to move his frogs. Tonight. Can we keep them for a while? Until he can find the right ponds for them?"

Silence. Lucas peers at Minna.

"May I ask one question?" says her mother.

"What?"

"How many frogs?"

Minna takes the phone away from her ear. How many frogs, she mouths. Lucas shrugs his shoulders.

"A great many," Minna says into the phone. "Mother?" she adds suddenly.

"Yes?"

"I wrote you a letter."

"I know," says her mother. "Eliza Moon, what a fine name. No matter. Bring the frogs."

FOURTEEN

Minna sleeps a dream-filled sleep. Scenes crowd in on her: Willie arriving at Lucas's house to help carry the tanks, eight in all, filled with frogs. "Why are we doing this?" asks Willie, whose practice has been interrupted. He pauses on the stairway. "And who's the man here in the picture who looks something like this big one?" Willie points his chin at the largest frog. "Who told him?" says Lucas, laughing. "I didn't," says Twig. "Honestly!" The taxi driver, wide-eyed, as they load four tanks in with Minna. Lucas goes with Twig and Willie and the rest of the tanks in the big car, Minna laughing out loud at the look of terror on Willie's face as Twig speeds out into traffic. "She's something, isn't she?" says the taxi driver admiringly, whistling between his teeth, one hand on a glass tank beside him. The moon is up, a large yellow globe above Minna's house, when they reach there. Minna's mother and father, McGrew, and Emily Parmalee help carry in the tanks. Willie exclaims over her father's record collection; the taxi driver fixes the drip in her mother's kitchen faucet and shows her how to make coffee with a pinch of cinnamon added to the grounds. Lucas puts his hand on the back of Minna's neck as they watch the frogs in her mother's writing room. "I like the frogs," announces Minna's mother. "Each has a different character. You see, that one's morose, and that one has a sly look. *Morose and Sly,* a good title." McGrew tapes an old headline he's been saving over a tank: SCIENTIST SAYS MADNESS PASSED BY VIRUS. All of them crowd into the dining room. There is a smell of cinnamon in the air. "Thank you," says Minna to her mother, who, like Willie, returns the gift. "Thank *you,*" says her mother.

"Call me if you get your vibrato," whispers Lucas as they leave.

The next few days pass quickly, blending into one another like the layers of Mrs. Pratt's trifle dessert. Miss Barbizon does not like Minna's sentence of vocabulary words. She passes it back with a tight mouth, raised eyebrows, and a low grade. Minna doesn't mind. Her head is filled with Mozart.

McGrew and Minna's father come to an agreement about baseball.

"I can't help you anymore," says Minna's father, slowly, painfully lowering himself onto the couch in his study. He looks at McGrew. "It is not, after all, my chosen profession."

"It is not mine either," says McGrew happily.

"It may be mine," says Emily Parmalee thoughtfully.

The frogs splash contentedly in her mother's writing room. When her mother types they are quiet, as if they wait for words to be strung together into a story. Once, when Minna looks in, her mother is reading out loud. Dozens of eyes watch her.

Minna practices. Though she knows the music well there are times when Mozart surprises her, moments when he creeps up with a phrase like a whispered secret that she has never before heard. *Aha, Wolfgang, you rascal.*

"How are you?" asks Lucas on the phone.

"No vibrato," says Minna.

"What about the frogs?"

"They don't have vibratos either," says Minna. *Two days.*

Silently they file into the concert hall for rehearsal, following Porch and Mrs. Willoughby-Fiske down the main aisle, through the stage door, and into the cavern behind.

"Here is the waiting room," announces Mrs. Willoughby-Fiske in a ponderous tone. Serious business, this. "One hour," she tells them, raising one finger in the air as if the word "one" is not sufficient.

They open their cases. Lucas takes out his rosin and tightens his bow. Imelda tunes nervously. Minna wipes her cello with a cloth. Orson fingers his strings.

"You're a bit flat," says Porch to Imelda. "Up a little."

Then they walk onstage.

The stage is lighted, but there is a vast blackness where there will be faces in two days. The chairs and music stands are arranged in a semicircle.

"I think it is time to meet each other again," says Porch with a smile. "Though I'll admit," he adds, "that you played great Mozart in your corners."

They sit, looking at each other nervously, as if together for the first time. Minna places her music on the stand. She searches for a crack in the floor for her end pin.

"Now." Porch stands in front of them. "I will not be here yelling at you, or stepping on your foot." He looks sideways at Orson. "Imelda, you will begin them."

Imelda looks up with a start.

"And remember," warns Porch, "play no matter what. Someone may cough, or a child may cry. A string may break. Your music may fall off the stand. Play on!"

Silence.

Porch grins suddenly. Then he jumps off the stage, disappearing into the seats.

Minna looks out into the darkness. She sees only tiny lights above the exit doors. She looks up into the balcony and decides to make her peace with Mozart.

> *Are you there, Wolfgang? I have come*
> *to know you very well, better than you know me.*
> *If you knew me, after all, you would have*
> *sent me a vibrato. But, no matter, as my mother*
> *Mrs. Pratt says. Your music doesn't really need*
> *a vibrato.*
>
> > *Minna*
>
> *P.S. If you do send one, make it during the*
> *andante.*

Imelda lifts her bow and looks at them.

"This is not cozy," she says suddenly. "I now know why Paganini could only compose music with a blanket over his head."

There is silence, then laughter.

"Play," says Imelda softly.

It is startling to hear the music in this space. The sound does not bounce about as it does in the rehearsal room. It does not escape into the carpet and curtains of Minna's room as it does when she practices at home. Here it seems to lift and then disappear, the notes gone, one after another, into the dark.

An hour passes quickly. They play through once with Porch's voice calling from the dark, even though he has said he won't.

"Legato, there, Minna . . . Crescendo, remember! . . . Pianissimo for the last three bars of the coda, Orson. You're too loud."

Then they play it through alone. When they are finished Porch's face appears below them over the edge of the stage.

"Splendid. You could play the presto with your eyes closed, I bet."

They smile at each other and do it for Porch then, as a final gift, their eyes clamped shut, Minna grinning.

Porch teaches them how to stand and bow from the waist together. He conducts them like a symphony.

"You play well together. You must take your final bow well together."

He beams.

One day.

FIFTEEN

"*I* will miss them," says Minna's mother about the frogs. "Especially these two."

"They like music," says Minna's father.

"They *love* my stories," says her mother wistfully.

Lucas smiles.

"It's time they went into the pond, where they'll be happy. They're growing up."

Minna's mother lifts her eyebrows at him.

Lucas has this day freed most of the frogs. Minna counts nine remaining, counting Morose and Sly, her mother's favorites. Minna, Lucas, and Willie have driven with Twig to park ponds around the city, Willie refusing to sit in front.

"Slow down here, Twig," he calls out from the backseat. "For heaven's sake!"

"My mother says Twig drives in a brisk manner," says Lucas.

"Hush up, the two of you, or drive yourself," answers Twig, having it out with a taxi driver who suddenly looks over, brakes, and grins at her.

Three park ponds in all they've visited, Lucas gently pushing the frogs to the edges. He does not seem sad, not even angry at his parents.

"They're going to give us a reception backstage after the competition," he says. "Win or lose, they say. That's a bit of a fuss, don't you think? For them."

Minna nods.

"Lucas?" she says, staring at the water. She can see their reflections there. "You wanted them to find the frogs. Didn't you?"

There was a pause.

"Maybe," says Lucas finally. "I knew they would someday." He pushes a frog to the edge of the grass. "Go on. Into the pond, you alien creature."

The frog jumps in, making a small splash. Their reflections turn wavery.

"Only one alien creature left in your house now," says Minna, her arms around her knees.

"Who?" asks Lucas.

"You," says Minna.

Lucas smiles and takes the last two frogs out of their glass aquarium. Morose and Sly.

"Not so," says Lucas. "My father and mother yelled at each other this morning." Lucas looks pleased. "My father threw a book in the living room.

My mother said the frogs had heard me play more than they had." Lucas puts Morose and Sly on the grass by the water.

"They said I could keep these two," he says after a moment.

Minna looks up, surprised.

"But it is time to let them go," says Lucas, turning to look at Minna. "*My* choice," he adds.

Lucas smiles and in the silence, one after the other, the last of his frogs slip into the water and away.

The day. Minna has wished for sunlight, but the day is not sunny. It is not even nice. Minna wakes to sheets of rain against her window. Wind whips the small trees outside. She can barely see across the street. Minna slips out of bed, padding barefoot down the hall to her mother's writing room. The room, clean after the frogs' departure, is beginning to look cluttered again. Minna sees a laundry basket with an array of socks inside. She bends down to look more closely. She smiles. All the socks are white. No stripes. There is a strange comfort in that, and in the beginnings of another mess.

"Minna?" Her mother comes into the room. "Dad's driving you early. Nervous?"

Minna shakes her head.

They look at the shelves where the frogs have been. Then Minna looks at her mother's sign: FACT AND FICTION ARE DIFFERENT TRUTHS. There is some-

thing here I almost know, thinks Minna. I am beginning to remember.

"Minna," says her mother softly, holding out a
folded paper. "Read what came in the mail today."

Minna unfolds the letter and reads:

Dear Mrs. Pratt,
   I love your stories. I am wondering, are
they *all* lies?

                                    Regards,
                                    Robert

Minna smiles.

"What did you answer?" asks Minna after a moment.

"Dear Robert," begins her mother, "some of them
are and some of them are not. But they are *all* true."

Minna nods. She looks at her mother's typewriter
for a long time. She reaches out to touch the keys.

"How did you know?" she asks after a moment.

"A crooked *r*," says her mother. "I know my
typewriter very well. I also," she adds, putting her
arm around Minna, "know you and your truths
very well. Whatever name you use."

There is more comfort in the kitchen. Minna's
father has lost his glasses. He searches through the
rubble of the kitchen counter, in the drawers among
the silverware, as Minna's mother bangs into breakfast.

McGrew hums at the table as he eats his cereal. On his lap, out of sight of his parents, is a newspaper with the headline: HOUSEWIFE CAN'T STOP EATING CATERPILLARS.

The phone rings. McGrew answers.

"What?" he says, folding his newspaper into his literature book.

"It's Emily Parmalee," he says to them. "She wonders if she can wear cleats to the concert. They're new," he adds.

"No," says Minna's father, joyfully rescuing his glasses from the dish drainer. "Tell her plain old shoes will be fine."

"No," sings McGrew into the telephone and hangs up.

Breakfast is scorched scrambled eggs and orange juice with frozen lumps that haven't dissolved. Minna smiles all through it.

There are rumblings of thunder and lightning as Minna dresses for the concert. Minna bends down to give her cello a pat before she zips it into its canvas case. She hoists it on her hip and goes to meet her father.

Downstairs Emily Parmalee is wearing a blue dress to which she has sewn sequins in odd places. She wears old shoes and the largest diamond stud earrings that Minna has ever seen. Minna peers closely at them.

"Fake," says Emily. She hands Minna a sealed envelope. "McGrew and I have a special message in this envelope that you should read just before you play."

Minna smiles at both of them and puts it in her skirt pocket.

"Remember," sings McGrew.

"I'll remember."

"Ready?" asks her father. He takes her cello and picks up an umbrella.

"Ready," says Minna.

And they race outside into the storm.

Backstage is filled with noise and instruments and musicians wandering nervously with music in their hands. Mrs. Willoughby-Fiske is not smiling, though Porch is. He herds Minna over to Imelda, who is peering over someone's shoulder at the music.

"Oh my dear," says Imelda. "Haydn's Opus 20. Four flats!"

Lucas comes wearing a suit with the sleeves a bit short. He looks at Minna.

"Well?"

"No," says Minna. "No vibrato."

Orson appears with his hair sleeked and shiny like a bowling ball. Minna can see the shape of his head for the very first time.

The big windows of the waiting room rattle in the wind, and the lights dim for a moment, then are bright again. Everyone quiets.

Mrs. Willoughby-Fiske arrives with their numbers, a long tumble of pearls falling over her chest like a mountain climber's rope.

"You are number ten," she says, looking intently at each of them. She holds up two hands, ten fingers, then disappears to hold up other numbers to other quartets.

"Last," says Porch happily as he tunes Imelda's violin. "Good position. Memorable. Make sure that last chord is in tune!" He finishes with Imelda's violin and reaches for Minna's cello. "This weather is not terrific for tuning," he mutters to her. "I'll tune you now, but I'll be out front. You'll have to make sure that you stay tuned."

A rush of wind and rain hits the windows and they all look up. Someone laughs nervously. Another in the corner bursts into tears. She has lost her music. There is a flurry of talk. Someone rushes out.

"Good-bye, good luck," says Porch, and before they can say anything he is gone.

"Number one," intones Mrs. Willoughby-Fiske and the room quiets. She holds up one finger.

It is time.

The room is eerily silent except for the wind and rain and the crashes of thunder with lightning afterward. The lights flicker.

"There was lightning and thunder just as Beethoven died," says Imelda as they all walk to the window. "It is said that he arose from his deathbed, shaking his fist at it, then he fell back dead."

"Thank you for that," says Orson, and they laugh.

Slowly, one after another, the quartets leave and return with bursts of talk.

"You were flat," says a violinist.

"I know," moans the cellist. "My end pin slipped. I nearly fell over my cello into the audience." Laughter.

"Lucas?" says Minna. They are leaning against the wall by the window, Minna's cello lying at her feet.

"What?" Lucas turns to look at her. His face is close to hers, so close that she can feel his breath on her cheek.

"Why are we doing this?"

Lightning flashes. The lights dim again. Lucas grins at her.

"Because we love it," he says simply.

"Have we always known that?" whispers Minna.

"Number ten," announces Mrs. Willoughby-Fiske.

They follow Mrs. Willoughby-Fiske out into the hall and through a dark hallway until they come to a door with a tiny window.

"Wait here," she says, "until I call you."

She opens the door and for a moment they hear the sound of music onstage. It is Haydn.

"Too slow," says Orson in a low voice. "At least we play to tempo."

Minna puts her hand in her skirt pocket and there, forgotten until now, is the envelope.

"Hold this," Minna whispers to Lucas, handing him her cello. "It's a note from Emily Parmalee and McGrew. They told me to open it just before we play."

Carefully, Minna opens the envelope. There is a folded sheet of paper inside. She holds it up to the exit light.

"What does it say?" asks Lucas.

"It says . . ." She grins suddenly. "It says . . ."

The door opens. Four silent musicians file out after Mrs. Willoughby-Fiske.

"Come now," she says to them.

"It says," repeats Minna, "the opera's not over 'til the fat lady sings."

They walk onstage smiling.

SIXTEEN

No one has prepared Minna for the applause. The noise surrounds her as she stands and bows with the others. Imelda and Orson look startled, too. Only Lucas stands calmly in the din, smiling slightly as if he awakens each day with it. They sit to the rustlings of the audience, the coughs, the sneezes. Minna sees her mother and father, Porch just in front, Emily Parmalee and McGrew smiling at her. Willie and Twig are on the aisle next to Mr. and Mrs. Ellerby. McGrew points down the row of seats and Minna looks. It is Lewis, the bus driver, wearing round glasses and a suit, studying his program.

Well, Wolfgang, well,
See what you have done. Look who has come
because of you.

Minna finds a crack in the wooden floor for her end pin. They tune softly, Lucas stopping to turn a peg. The lights dim, then brighten. The audience quiets. Imelda lifts her bow. There is a tiny beading of sweat on her upper lip. She nods. And they begin.

It is a bit like dying, Minna thinks, or so she's heard. All the things she must remember, all the things she has learned pass by in her mind's eye: the fortes, the pianissimos, the difficult bowing parts she has checked in pencil on her music, the fingering. She nearly forgets the first repeat, somehow. Lucas, next to her, looks at her and smiles because he knows it. The allegro ends, and someone in the balcony applauds and is quickly hushed by a sister, a brother, a wife. Imelda smiles. Orson tunes. Minna takes a breath. *The andante*. Minna waits through her measures of rests, looking out to find Porch. But she can't see him in the dark. Minna smiles at this; places her bow on the strings. Begins. Strangely, Minna thinks about it later, the andante seems to come from her fingers for the very first time, not from her head. Her fingers stretch without her telling them to stretch. They have learned the music. They know Mozart. Some hairs come loose from Orson's bow, and they trail like threads of silver in the light as he plays. She remembers to repeat. And then, two measures from the end of the coda, where Minna feels nearly safe, the lights go out.

There is a gasp from the audience, a bustle from backstage, a loud noise as something falls to the floor. A flashlight. The audience murmurs become louder as they finish the last chord of the coda.

No one says it. Not one of them asks what to do. They know. *Play no matter what.*

"Ready?" asks Imelda.

"Yes," says Orson.

A small light suddenly appears in the wings.

"Yes," says Lucas.

"Min?"

"Ready."

"Play," says Imelda.

They do not start together, but no one else knows. Three measures into the presto the audience quiets. Minna grins in the darkness. *You can play the presto with your eyes closed, I bet.* And they can. Lucas laughs once beside her, and at the last crescendo Minna thinks about the final two chords. *Play them in tune.* They do.

The applause comes at the same moment, surprising them all again. The lights come on—*too late or maybe not*—and they rise clumsily by their chairs. And it is over. The audience is on its feet, applauding and shouting. The house lights go on and at last Minna sees Porch, standing, too.

Lucas leans over close to Minna.

"Was that a small vibrato at the very end of the

andante?" he asks, his voice loud over the noise of the applause.

"No!" says Minna, grinning.

It is not until Mrs. Willoughby-Fiske barrels on-stage with bouquets of red roses, her pearls swinging murderously from side to side, that they realize that they have won.

They have, Porch tells them later, forgotten to take their final bow.

"The end was in tune, you know," says Minna backstage. "No one heard."

"I heard," says Porch fervently, his arm around her. "*I* heard!"

There is noise everywhere; platters of food and punch, and laughter. Minna's mother and father hug her. Mrs. Ellerby holds a moist handkerchief to her eyes. Mr. Ellerby kisses Lucas with a noisy kiss, causing Lucas's eyes to widen. Imelda's parents are there, her mother short and serious, her father with red hair. Everything they say seems important. Orson's parents come with his younger brothers, four smaller Orsons. One brother eats up the entire contents of a dish of chocolate truffles. Lewis waves at Minna. Emily Parmalee's sequins drop everywhere, like rice after a wedding.

"You didn't get your vibrato, did you?"

Minna turns.

"No," she says, smiling at McGrew.

"I didn't think so," says McGrew, matter-of-factly.

"McGrew?"

"What?"

"The note helped."

"I know," sings McGrew.

Lucas beckons to Minna and they walk out of the noise into the quiet hallway, where, tucked into the instrument cases and coats and umbrellas, Willie and Twig stand with their arms around each other.

". . . and in the evening," says Willie, "when Mama is asleep and the stars are out, I go out in the cornfield to play. The corn stalks are like an audience of music lovers, like the people on the street of the city. I can almost see the music winding down the rows, from stalk to stalk. Will you come with me? As soon as we have the money?"

"Yes," says Twig, reaching up to touch his hair. "As soon as we have the money."

Minna and Lucas stand there, not daring to move, as Willie and Twig kiss. They kiss for so long that finally, with a sigh, Lucas takes Minna by the hand and they leave.

Hidden behind the stage curtain, Minna takes out the envelope that Mrs. Willoughby-Fiske has given her. A one hundred dollar bill is tucked neatly inside.

"Tomorrow?" Minna says to Lucas.

Lucas nods.

"You'll have to do it," says Minna, handing him

the envelope. "He always gives me back the money."

"I'll do it," says Lucas. He takes his money out and adds it to Minna's. "For Twig," he says. "Now they can both go."

They walk into the hallway again, where everyone is leaving.

"Good–bye, luv," says Minna's mother to Mrs. Ellerby.

"Good–bye, luv," echoes Mrs. Ellerby, startling herself.

"Call if you get a vibrato," whispers Lucas to Minna.

The house is still when Minna wakes in the night. But it is not dark. Moonlight streams in the window. It falls across her bed and onto the rug, and touches the mirror on the wall. For a while Minna watches it. Then, suddenly, she leans over the edge of the bed to touch her cello, lying by her bed like a sleep-over guest. She plucks a string. Slowly she sits up, sliding out from under the covers. She picks up her cello and bow and pulls a wooden chair over into her closet. She adjusts her end pin and tightens her bow. She pulls the light cord so that the light goes on above her. She begins to play, very softly at first, then a bit louder. Minna smiles at the new rich sound. She turns to watch her hand, vibrating on the strings. Finally, after a while, she stops, sitting silently in the lighted closet. She reaches up and turns off the light. She lays the cello by the bed again, the bow across it, and slips back under the covers. For a moment she doesn't move. She lies there staring in the moonlight. She looks at the clock on her night table. Twelve thirty. She hesitates, then picks up the phone and dials.

On the first ring a phone is lifted.

"Congratulations," says Lucas.